FOCUS ON SUCCESS

Ausgabe Technik

Workbook

5th edition

von
Michael Benford
Michael Macfarlane
Isobel Williams
Steve Williams

unter Mitarbeit der Verlagsredaktion

Vokabeltrainer-App
*Verfügbar für: iOS, Android
und Windows Phone*

Verfasser/innen:

Michael Benford, Bochum
Michael Macfarlane, Oxford
Isobel Williams, Berlin
Steve Williams, Corio Bay Media

Projektleitung: Andreas Goebel
Verlagsredaktion: Kari-ann Warnakulasuriya
Außenredaktion: Katinka Welz, Ingolstadt
Redaktionelle Mitarbeit: Elise Nelson
Umschlaggestaltung: Klein & Halm Grafikdesign, Berlin
Layout und technische Umsetzung: Oxana Rödel, Absatz DTP-Service, Teltow
Coverfoto: Shutterstock / Mikhail Zahranichny
Illustrationen: Oxford Designers & Illustrators

Erhältlich sind auch:

Schülerbuch	ISBN 978-3-06-451085-2
Handreichungen zum Unterricht mit Unterrichtsmanager (UM) und 3 Audio-CDs	ISBN 978-3-06-451087-6
Unterrichtsmanager Premium (DVD)	ISBN 978-3-06-451088-3
Vocabulary practice book	ISBN 978-3-06-451079-1
Vokabeltrainer-App für Android, Apple oder Windows	In dem jeweiligen App Store

Soweit in diesem Lehrwerk Personen fotografisch abgebildet sind und ihnen von der Redaktion fiktive Namen, Berufe, Dialoge und Ähnliches zugeordnet oder diese Personen in bestimmte Kontexte gesetzt werden, dienen diese Zuordnungen und Darstellungen ausschließlich der Veranschaulichung und dem besseren Verständnis des Inhalts.

www.cornelsen.de

Die Webseiten Dritter, deren Internetadressen in diesem Lehrwerk angegeben sind, wurden vor Drucklegung sorgfältig geprüft. Der Verlag übernimmt keine Gewähr für die Aktualität und den Inhalt dieser Seiten oder solcher, die mit ihnen verlinkt sind.

1. Auflage, 2. Druck 2018

Alle Drucke dieser Auflage sind inhaltlich unverändert und können im Unterricht nebeneinander verwendet werden.

© 2015 Cornelsen Schulverlage GmbH, Berlin
© 2018 Cornelsen Verlag GmbH, Berlin

Druck: Athesiadruck GmbH

ISBN 978-3-06-451086-9

PEFC zertifiziert
Dieses Produkt stammt aus nachhaltig bewirtschafteten Wäldern und kontrollierten Quellen.
www.pefc.de
PEFC/18-31-166

CONTENTS

1 The cult of celebrity

1 TALKING ABOUT CELEBRITY

Underline twelve English words you can use when you talk about celebrities. The words are all on pages 6 and 7 of the student's book.

UPFFANSMXOPAPARAZZIGRLFAMOUSTSTATUSYSTARPLUXURYMLLEGENDZUSTALKERPKACTORMIMAGELBKMAUTOGRAPHCPOPULARITY

2 GETTING IT RIGHT

→ Position of adverbs of time, SB S. 273

Choose the correct position (A or B) for the adverb of time in the brackets.

1 John **A** spends too much money **B** on fan articles. (always)
2 The paparazzi **A** wait for celebrities **B** outside clubs and bars. (usually)
3 **A** I **B** read about celebrities' problems in the newspapers. (regularly)
4 My favourite singer **A** performs **B** in my town. (never)
5 The group is **A** on the radio **B**. (every day)
6 Celebrities **A** love to see their name in the news **B**. (usually)
7 Paparazzi **A** get very rich **B** with their photos. (sometimes)
8 Some stars **A** are **B** on tour. (always)

3 GETTING IT RIGHT

→ Simple present, SB S. 249

Complete the story using the verbs in brackets in the simple present. Take care with questions and negatives.

Briony and Holly Banks ___are___ ¹ (be) twins. They both _____ ²
(love) to dance and they _____ ³ (have) a lot of talent. They
_____ ⁴ (enter) a talent show competition.

On the night of the show, Briony _____ ⁵ (see) that her sister
_____ ⁶ (not be happy). 'What _____ ⁷ (be)
the problem, Holly?' she _____ ⁸ (ask). 'I _____ ⁹
(be scared),' Holly _____ ¹⁰ (tell) her.
When the girls _____ ¹¹ (come) on stage, one of the judges
_____ ¹² (smile) kindly. 'Just _____ ¹³ (relax),' he _____ ¹⁴ (say). Holly suddenly _____ ¹⁵
(feel) great and she and her sister _____ ¹⁶ (win) the competition.

4 ASKING QUESTIONS

→ Simple present, SB S. 249; Question words, SB S. 222

Read the answers a celebrity fashion model gave during a TV interview in London. Use the correct forms of *be* and *do* together with the question words from the box to complete the interviewer's questions. Use each question word only once.

How ■ What ■ When ■ Where ■ Who ■ Why

1 _____ your name?   *My name is Willow.*

2 _____ you from?   *I'm from New York.*

3	_____ you like London?	*I love London.*
4	_____ you in London today?	*I'm in London today to model some clothes.*
5	_____ you usually start work?	*I usually start work at 6 am.*
6	_____ your favourite designer?	*My favourite designer is Marco.*

5 BUILDING SKILLS

→ Vorbereitung auf das Lesen, SB S. 214

Before you read the text below, study the clues on the page and then choose the best ending to complete the following statement.

The article is about a celebrity who
- **a** believes the media are always nice to her because she is famous.
- **b** knows from experience that being a celebrity is not always fun.
- **c** pays reporters and paparazzi to give her the attention she wants.

SKILLS CHECKLIST: Predicting

☑ Have I read the title?
☑ Have I looked at the photo?
☑ Have I read the caption under the photo?

FAME – IS IT WORTH IT?

A lot of stories about Desirée, last month's winner of *Stars for Tomorrow*, are appearing in the tabloid newspapers at the moment. Talking openly to *Fame and Fortune* magazine, the slim, sexy singer explains why media attention is not always a good thing.

5 'Everybody is talking about my relationship with Patrick Strong, one of the judges on the show,' she says. 'I know that when you're a celebrity, you have to give up a lot of your private life. The fans want to know what you're doing,' she says. 'Sometimes things appear in the papers that you don't like, but you learn to accept it. Say you're having a bad day, and
10 someone takes your picture and sells it to the media, that's part of the life of a celebrity,' she continues.

'Some of the stories appearing in the press at the moment are just too personal, though. Now that Patrick and I are close, I'm scared to leave the house because I know the reporters and the paparazzi are
15 waiting for me. They are making my life hard at the moment.'

(182 words)

'You know that the media is interested in your private life when you're a celebrity, but I did not expect it to be this bad.'

6 LOOKING AT THE TEXT

→ Rezeption: Leseverstehen, SB S. 214

Say if these statements are true (T) or false (F). Correct the wrong statements.

1 Desirée is currently appearing in *Stars for Tomorrow*.
☐ _____

2 Desirée knows Patrick well because he is her cousin.
☐ _____

3 Desirée understands that her fans are interested in her.
☐ _____

4 She does not want paparazzi to take photos when she is looking bad. ☐ _____ _____ _____

5 The media is full of reports about Desirée's professional plans at the moment. ☐ _____ _____ _____

6 Desirée is unhappy about the attention the press is giving her at the moment. ☐ _____ _____ _____

7 GETTING IT RIGHT

→ Present progressive, SB S. 249

A Complete the transcript of a phone call between Desirée and Patrick with the words and phrases in brackets. Put the verbs in the present progressive.

Desirée Hi Patrick.

Patrick Hi Desirée. I ___*am calling*___ [1] (call) from my car. What _____ [2] (you do) at the moment?

Desirée I _____ [3] (read) the latest report about us in the newspaper.

Patrick What story _____ [4] (the press make up) now?

Desirée That you _____ [5] (date) another woman.

Patrick These people _____ [6] (go too far). _____ [7] (they try) to split us up?

Desirée I suppose they _____ [8] (only do) their job. Oh, no! Two reporters _____ [9] (walk up) the path to the front door.

Patrick Don't worry, darling. I _____ [10] (drive into) your street right now. I can see them.

B Listen and check.

8 GETTING IT RIGHT

→ Simple present ■ Present progressive, SB S. 249

Choose the simple present or the present progressive to complete the extract from Desirée's fan blog.

I *work / am working* [1] on a new album and everything *goes / is going* [2] well at the moment. OK, I *have / am having* [3] some trouble with the press. The paparazzi *stalk / are stalking* [4] me from morning till night and some reporters *look / are looking* [5] in the window right now. So what? I *know / am knowing* [6] that none of you *believe / are believing* [7] the stories in the papers. I *love / am loving* [8] you all.

Desirée ♥

1 TALKING ABOUT SPORT

A Unscramble the letters to make words and expressions to talk about sport. Some letters have already been given. All the words and expressions are on page 12 of the student's book.

1 cipainpratt   P R ☐ ☐ C ☐ ☐ ☐ ☐ T

2 acesportt   ☐ E ☐ T ☐ ☐ ☐ R

3 labofolt   ☐ O ☐ ☐ A ☐ ☐

4 alpy nestin   ☐ ☐ A ☐ ☐ ☐ N ☐ ☐

5 proustp a meat   ☐ ☐ P ☐ ☐ ☐ ☐ A ☐ E ☐ ☐

6 peek-ift avicetisit   ☐ ☐ E ☐ - ☐ ☐ ☐ ☐ A ☐ ☐ ☐ ☐ ☐ T ☐ ☐ S

7 od cabeiors   ☐ O ☐ ☐ R ☐ ☐ ☐ C ☐

8 og gigjong   ☐ ☐ ☐ ☐ O ☐ ☐ ☐ G

B Complete the dialogue with six of the words/expressions.

A Hello, Ben. I haven't seen you for ages. How are you? You look very well. Do you still do your

_____ ¹?

B Yes. I _____ ² at the gym twice a week and I _____ ³

in the park every morning. I took part in a charity run last Saturday. That's the first time I've been a

_____ ⁴ in an event like that. It was a lot of fun. But what about you? You used

to be very keen on _____ ⁵. Do you still play for a team?

A No. I sometimes kick a ball around with my mates, but I stopped playing seriously ages ago. I still

go to matches, but I'm only a _____ ⁶ these days. I prefer to watch other people

doing the hard work.

2 GETTING IT RIGHT

→ Simple past, SB S. 251

Complete the sentences with the simple past form of the underlined verb. Be careful with irregular forms.

1 I normally go to the gym twice a week. Last week, I only _____ once.

2 We usually play tennis outside. Yesterday, we _____ in the hall.

3 The team doesn't often win their matches, but they _____ last Saturday.

4 The match usually begins at 3 pm, but last week it _____ at 3.30 pm.

5 Where did you buy your running shoes? I _____ them at RunFast.

6 Did you take part in the event this year? Yes. I _____ as usual.

3 GETTING IT RIGHT

→ Present perfect, SB S. 253

A Use the correct form of the verb in brackets to complete the sentences. Circle the signal words.

1 Claire _has left_ ¹ (leave) our swimming club. She _____ ² (just move) to
another town.

2 Paul _____ ¹ (not arrive) yet. He _____ ²
(never be) late for a game before.

3 _____¹ (you / hear) the news already? Mark Miller _____

_____² (just join) our local ice hockey team.

4 _____¹ (you / meet) our new player, Jan, yet? She _____²

(play) squash in competitions all over the country.

B Complete the expressions with *for* or *since*. → *For, since,* SB S. 254

1	_____ six years	5	_____ last week
2	_____ a long time	6	_____ we moved to Berlin
3	_____ Easter	7	_____ 21 June
4	_____ a couple of hours	8	_____ ever

4 **GETTING IT RIGHT** → Simple past ■ Present perfect, SB S. 254

Cross out the incorrect version of the verb to complete the text. Circle the expressions that helped you decide. The first one has been done for you.

(Earlier today), the Anti-Doping Agency charged / has charged¹ another sports personality with using performance-enhancing drugs. Up till now, the agency did not say / has not said² who the celebrity sportsperson is. According to an insider, however, people from the agency searched / have searched³ the home of one of the country's top runners earlier this week.

The runner, who won / has won⁴ a lot of prizes during his career, told / has told⁵ us in a telephone interview yesterday, that he and another runner only drank / have drunk⁶ a fruit juice before the event. The fruit-juice company sponsored / has sponsored⁷ both runners for over two years. This morning, in a press conference, a spokesperson for the company said / has said⁸: 'Doping in sport was / has been⁹ a problem for years but the drinks we gave / have given¹⁰ the runners before the race were / have been¹¹ pure fruit juice, as always. None of our drinks ever contained / have ever contained¹² drugs.'

5 **GETTING IT RIGHT** → Pronouns, SB S. 268

A Complete each message using a subject or an object pronoun for the underlined words.

EXAMPLE: There is a message from your parents on the answering machine.
Can you listen to ___*it*___ and call ___*them*___ back?

1 Joe is working late and can't come to football practice.

Can you call _____ at the office?

2 I am playing in a hockey team at the moment.

Would you like you to watch _____ play?

3 Clara knows you have some new tennis balls.

_____¹ would like to borrow _____².

4 We have a problem with the CD player.

Can you help _____¹ fix _____²?

5 Some people say that Zumba is fun. Jessica and I are going to try Zumba.

_____¹ say that Zumba is fun. _____² are going to try _____³.

B Read Ann's blog post about her dance class and find the pronouns. Highlight the subject pronouns in yellow, the object pronouns in green and the possessive adjectives in blue. The first three have been done for you. Now you only have to find 24 more.

Here's some news about my dance class. We have a new instructor. Her name is Alice. She's a really good teacher. Dancing is a great way to keep fit and have fun. It's also a great way to meet people. There are ten of us in the class. A few weeks ago, a boy called Tim had a
5 problem with one of his shoes. Its *sole* [Sohle] broke and this made him fall and crash into me. Those of you who follow this blog know that I've always liked him, but this was the first time he noticed me. It wasn't long till we started going out. His parents have invited us to visit them next weekend in their new home. They have just moved to Glasgow.
10 If you want to join the dance class, send me your email address.

6 BUILDING SKILLS

→ Rezeption: Hörverstehen, SB S. 225

A You are going to listen to three people talk about how they keep fit. Before you listen, look at the photos and study the questions on the notepad below. Then choose the expressions from this list that you think you will hear.

1 strengthens the heart and the lungs
2 no fun at all
3 reduce stress
4 a fun way to keep fit
5 exercise every bit of your body
6 get slim and stay slim
7 it's really boring
8 helps you relax
9 gives you a good feeling

Jane, 26, teacher   Will, 22, trainee   Lily, 18, student

Who	What?	Where?	Health benefits?	Other?
Jane, 26, teacher	_____ _____ 1	in class; at _____ 2	good for _____, _____ 3, muscles; gets rid of _____ 4	fun; not _____ 5
Will, 22, trainee	_____ _____ 1	_____ _____ 2	great _____ 3; relaxing / you _____ 4; losing _____ 5	swimming helps you get _____ 6
Lily, 18, student	_____ _____ 1	_____ _____ 2	even if you _____ 3 you feel great; _____ 4 the calories; working with _____ 5 = good feeling	team sport good way to _____ 6; made _____ 7

B Now listen and check.
3

C Before you listen again, use information from the page to fill in the notepad with as much information as you can. Then listen again and complete the notes.
3

1 TALKING ABOUT BRANDS

A Translate the words into English to complete the crossword with words you can use to talk about brands. All the words are on pages 18 and 19 of the student's book.

ACROSS:
1 Werbespruch
2 modisch
4 Ware
5 erschwinglich
6 Qualität
9 Wahl

DOWN:
3 Preis
7 Werbung
8 Werte
10 berühmt

B Unscramble the highlighted letters in the crossword to make a two-word expression which says what shoppers often look for.

☐☐☐☐☐ ☐☐☐☐☐

2 GETTING IT RIGHT

→ Adjectives ▪ Adverbs of manner, SB S. 270

A Adjective or adverb? Underline the correct form.

1 If you don't have much money, you have to shop careful / carefully.
2 Don't simple / simply buy something because it's been advertised by a star.
3 The clothes look beautiful / beautifully when they're on a model.
4 It is usual / usually safer to buy a brand-name computer.
5 These jeans look similar / similarly to the ones I saw advertised last week.
6 Expensive / expensively products don't always last longer than goods you buy cheap / cheaply.

B Underline the adverbs below then unscramble the words to make sentences. Make sure you put the adverbs in the correct positions.

1 at the outlet store / frequently / Lucy / shops

_____

2 always / dresses / Jim / well

_____

3 my new computer / stopped / suddenly / working

_____

4 good / in that café / is / the coffee / usually

_____

5 I / these boots / really / want

_____

3 **USING A DICTIONARY**   → Ein Wörterbuch benutzen, SB S. 217; Vokabeln lernen, SB S. 220

Complete the table using your dictionary. The words are from page 19 of the student's book.

Noun	Verb	Adjective
choice	_____ 1	_____ 2
cost	_____ 3	_____ 4
_____ 5	_____ 6	affordable

4 **GETTING IT RIGHT**   → Comparison of adjectives and adverbs, SB S. 271

A Joe is shopping for a new smartphone. Use information from the table to complete his thoughts with the correct form of the words in brackets. Add *as … as* or *… than* where necessary.

	Universe	NeatPhone	Bright
dimensions	142mm × 73mm × 8.1mm	124mm × 59mm × 7.6mm	160mm × 84mm × 8.4mm
weight	145gr	112gr	206gr
battery life	+++++	+++	++++
price	€650	€600	€585

Oh, dear. I'm not sure which of these three phones to choose. I can see that the Universe is _bigger than_ [1]

(big) the NeatPhone and the Bright is the _biggest_ [2] (big) of all three, but I'll have to think some more.

How heavy are they? The NeatPhone is _____ [3] (light) the two other phones. The

Universe is not _____ [4] (heavy) the Bright. The Bright is _____ [5]

(heavy) the other two.

What does it say here about the battery life? The battery life

of the NeatPhone is not _____ [6] (long) the battery

life of the Bright. It looks as if the batteries of the Universe

last _____ [7] (long).

What about the price? Well, the Bright is the _____ [8]

(cheap) of the phones. The NeatPhone is _____

_____ [9] (expensive) the Bright, and

the Universe is the _____ [10] (expensive)

of them all. Oh, I don't know which of these three phones is _____ [11] (good). Choosing a phone is one

of the _____ [12] (difficult) things to do in life. Hmmm. I think I'll buy the …

B Now listen and check.

C Listen again. Which phone does Joe choose and why?

5 COLLOCATIONS

→ Ein Wörterbuch benutzen, SB S. 217

Cross out the word which you cannot use to form a collocation with the word in capital letters.

1 current ▪ high ▪ latest ▪ low ▪ newest FASHION
2 famous ▪ leading ▪ popular ▪ victim ▪ well-known BRAND
3 best ▪ good ▪ poor ▪ new ▪ top QUALITY
4 blue ▪ copies ▪ designer ▪ skinny ▪ tight JEANS
5 DESIGNER clothes ▪ house ▪ jeans ▪ label ▪ name

6 BUILDING SKILLS

→ Interaktion: An Diskussionen teilnehmen, SB S. 246

A **How good is your knowledge of phrases for discussion? Without checking the back flap of the student's book, write at least one phrase for each heading.**

SKILLS CHECKLIST: Phrases for discussions

☑ Have I learned suitable phrases for discussion?
☑ Do I know how and when to use them?

Giving an opinion　　Giving reasons　　　　　Agreeing with an opinion

Disagreeing with an opinion　　Interrupting

B **Circle the correct word in brackets to complete the sentences.**

1 My own (reason / view) of the matter is that it's fun to wear the latest fashions.
2 In my (meaning / opinion), the style doesn't suit everyone.
3 The main (reason / idea) is that the clothes are too expensive for teenagers.
4 I'm sorry, but I have to (agree / disagree) with you on that point. Expensive T-shirts don't always last longer than cheap ones.
5 I'm (afraid / concerned) I can't accept that. A designer watch will last forever.
6 Can I just (interrupt / tell) you for a moment? I strongly (agree / believe) that you have to spend money to look good.

C **Imagine that you are going to take part in a discussion about whether to buy designer or regular jeans and why. Complete the cards with arguments for and against designer jeans and regular jeans.**

Designer jeans		Regular jeans	
for	**against**	**for**	**against**
fit better, …	*expensive, …*	*inexpensive, …*	*poor quality, …*

D **Now decide on your point of view and make some notes that you could use in a discussion on the question.**

Jeans are jeans. The only difference is the name.

Designer jeans last longer and fit better.

SKILLS CHECKLIST: Group discussions

☑ Have I thought about what I want to say?
☑ Have I prepared some bullet points?
☑ Have I written down key phrases in English?

E **If you have the chance, carry out the discussion with two or three other people. Check with your teacher if you can do this in class.**

4 Leisure and free time

1 TALKING ABOUT FREE TIME ACTIVITIES

Complete the mindmap with free time activities.

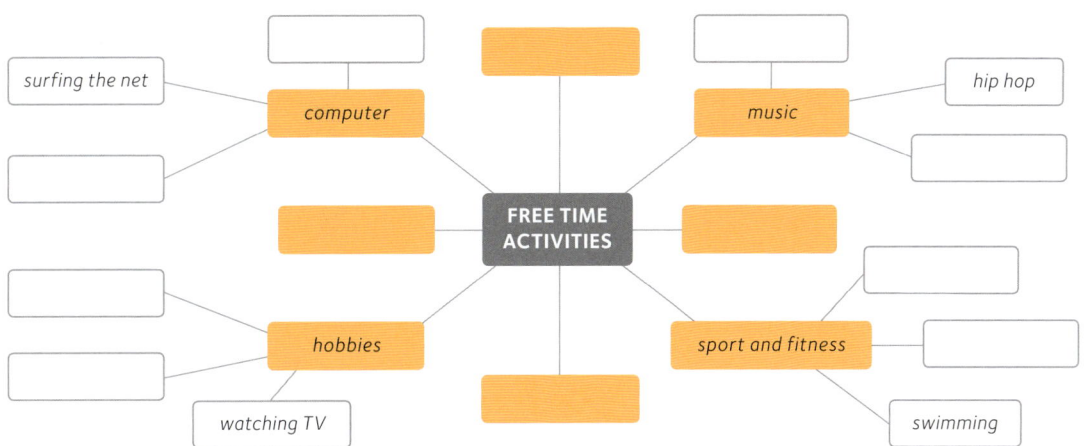

2 GETTING IT RIGHT

→ *Will* future ▪ *Going to* future, SB S. 257

A Fill in the correct form of the *will* future.

1 **A** _____¹ (you come) with me to the pop festival tomorrow?

   B Probably not. The weather reporter said there _____² (probably be)
   a storm in the evening.

   A Oh, no! I hope it _____³ (not be) stormy. If it is, the organizers

   _____⁴ (cancel) the festival.

2 **A** It's disco night at the youth club. _____⁵ (I see) you there later?

   B No, I _____⁶ (not have) time this evening. I have to do my homework.

   A Come on! I _____⁷ (help) you. Then we _____⁸
   (be able to) go together.

B Use the notes to make sentences using the *going to* future.

EXAMPLE: Jane / join / salsa class / this winter   *Jane is going to join a salsa class this winter.*

1 I / train for / next marathon

   _____

2 Mark and Mindy / go backpacking / Australia / next summer

   _____

3 some pupils / start / film club / next term

   _____

4 snooker championships / be held / Paris / this year

   _____

5 you / really / buy / motorbike?

   _____

6 I / not go shopping / for the rest of the year

   _____

13

3 **BUILDING SKILLS** → Produktion: Cartoons beschreiben und analysieren, SB S. 236

A **Choose the correct words from the brackets to complete the description of the cartoon.**

The cartoon shows a teenage boy and his mother in a living room. The boy _____¹ (is lying / lies) on the sofa. He _____² (has / is) overweight. He _____

_____³ (is looking / looks) frightened because a group of *vultures* [Geier] _____⁴

(are watching / watch) him _____⁵

(hungry / hungrily). Through the open window, we can see that two more vultures _____⁶

(fly / are flying) to join their friends. The boy's mother

_____⁷ (stands / is standing) behind her son. She appears to be _____⁸

(angry / angrily). She _____⁹ (shouts / is shouting) the words that are written under the cartoon.

"Maybe if you showed some sign of life once in a while this sort of thing wouldn't happen."

B **Complete the interpretation of the cartoon with one of the sentence endings below.**

The joke is that …
a mothers don't understand anything about relaxing.
b some kids are so lazy that they appear to be dead.
c some vultures have come to eat an overweight boy.

4 **LOOKING AT THE TEXT** → Rezeption: Leseverstehen, SB S. 214

Jenny, 16, often uses her blog to talk about her problems with her parents.

Read the post and say if the following statements are true (T) or false (F).

1 Jenny enjoys listening to how her parents behaved when they were teenagers. ☐

2 She doesn't use any social networks. ☐

3 She likes to meet her friends outside after school. ☐

4 According to Jenny, you can find out about a lot of things on the Internet. ☐

5 She doesn't want to have contact with people online. ☐

6 She would like the older generation to be more tolerant towards teenagers. ☐

'When I was your age …'

How often have you heard this in the last few weeks? You're chilling, lying on the sofa, listening to music or checking some post and – bang! – all the good feelings disappear and you have to listen to how life was in the old days. Everybody wrote letters and if you wanted to chat, you sat on the step and spoke to the kids next door. So what? History is interesting, but things change and develop. →

Kids today use social networking. I don't have to be with my friends in person to have a conversation, I can video call them. I don't need go to my mate's house and tell him about a great new band, I can post a link to it in our Facebook group.

It's not all about having fun. We also use social networking to discuss schoolwork and to exchange ideas. We are open to other people's ideas and enjoy mixing with people from different groups.

I wish people would just understand that things are different today. I mean, when my parents and grandparents were growing up they didn't even have computers!

Perhaps, when older people start a sentence with, 'When I was your age …' they should try to end it with the words, 'I was a teenager, too.'

(214 words)

5 BUILDING SKILLS

→ Schriftliche Mediation, SB S. 240

Ein Freund hat Ihnen erzählt, dass seine Mutter ständig zu ihm sagt: „Als ich in deinem Alter war…!". Schreiben Sie eine E-Mail an diesen Freund und erzählen Sie ihm von Jennys Blog aus Übung 4, und erläutern Sie Jennys Anregungen zu diesem Thema.

> **SKILLS CHECKLIST: Written mediation**
>
> ☑ Have I read the situation?
> ☑ Have I understood who the mediation is for?
> ☑ Have I written the right sort of text?

6 GETTING IT RIGHT

→ Quantifiers, SB S. 274

Choose the correct words from the brackets to complete the dialogues.

1 **A** Did you see _____[1] (any / some) interesting programmes on TV last night?

 B I don't watch _____[2] (many / much) TV. I do so many other things and there's too _____[3] (few / little) time to fit everything in.

2 **A** I go to the gym _____[4] (a few / a little) times a week. What about you?

 B I go to the gym, too. There are often _____[5] (any / some) interesting people there.

3 **A** Does your college offer _____[6] (many / much) after-school activities?

 B No, they don't offer _____[7] (any / some). Not _____[8] (many / much) people are interested.

4 **A** We have _____[9] (a few / a little) time before the dance class starts. Can you show me _____[10] (any / some) moves?

 B If you like. How _____[11] (many / much) moves do you know already?

 A Not _____[12] (many / much). I've only been here _____[13] (a few / a little) times and I don't practise _____[14] (many / much) at home.

7 BUILDING SKILLS

→ Produktion: Bilder beschreiben und analysieren, SB S. 236

Describe the photo, relating it to the topic of the unit. Explain why you would (not) enjoy the activity shown.

> **SKILLS CHECKLIST: Describing a picture**
>
> ☑ Have I described the people in the picture?
> ☑ Have I described the atmosphere?

5 The virtual world

1 WORKING WITH WORDS

Fill in the gaps with some of the highlighted words from the text on pages 36 and 37 of the student's book.

_____[1] of how old you are – you can be a child or an _____[2] –

you're never too old to open a social media account. There are _____[3] to choose from,

e.g. Facebook, Twitter, LinkedIn or Instagram. At first sight they _____[4] to be very different,

but they are the same in many ways. This is because they let people _____[5] with each other

and help them feel less cut off and _____[6].

A recent _____[7] conducted by an online bank has shown that on _____[8], Britons

spend at least one hour on the Internet per day. In some cases, the amount of time spent on social media

_____[9] two hours. For these reasons, many people open a social media account to

_____[10] being forgotten by their friends.

2 LOOKING AT THE TEXT

→ Rezeption: Leseverstehen, SB S. 214

Answer these questions on the text on pages 36 and 37 of the student's book in your own words.

1 How much time does the average British adult or child spend on social media every day?

_____

2 How are the social media habits of men and women different?

_____

3 How many Britons use Twitter for more than two hours a day?

_____

4 Which social media platform is most popular? How do we know?

_____

5 How do some people make sure they are not cut off from their friends?

_____

6 What is Rebecca Dye's job?

_____

7 What does Rebecca Dye probably mean when she says 'at the expense of other communications'?

_____

8 How will Rebecca Dye's company interact more with its customers in future?

_____

3 BUILDING SKILLS

→ Rezeption: Leseverstehen – Grobverständnis, SB S. 214

A Study the box on the right then skim the text and decide which of the following statements best summarizes it.

a Social media only played a small part in the volunteers' lives.

b Only the lonely use Facebook and Twitter.

c Giving up social media can make room for other things.

d Social media use is a bad habit that must be broken.

SKILLS CHECKLIST: Skimming

☑ Have I read the title carefully?
☑ Have I read all of the first paragraph?
☑ Have I read the first sentence of all the other paragraphs?
☑ Have I read all of the final paragraph?

FACEBOOK AND TWITTER ADDICTS GO 'COLD TURKEY' IN MAJOR EXPERIMENT

The research project focused on a month-long experiment where 40 people from across the UK were forced to change their normal social media behaviours. A number of Facebook and Twitter *addicts* suffered a range of *withdrawal symptoms* after being forced to deactivate their accounts for a month.

5   Many described extreme feelings of isolation because of the reduced contact with friends or family, while others said they were frustrated at losing their key communication tool. Some users lost contact with friends and family because they had no contact details other than a Facebook address.

As one female *volunteer* from Yorkshire *admitted*: 'So much of my life was organised via
10 Facebook. I haven't communicated with my family all week.' Another of the volunteers said: 'I've felt alone and cut off from the world. My fingers seem to be programmed to seek out the Facebook app every time I pick up my phone.'

Social media addicts had to find other ways to spend their time. A woman from Wales said being taken off Facebook had allowed her to focus on the household, while another volunteer
15 *confessed* the 'ban' had allowed her to spend more time with her daughter.   (195 words)

Vocabulary notes							
cold turkey	*kalter Entzug*	withdrawal symptoms	*Entzugserscheinungen*	to admit	*zugeben*		
addict	*Süchtige(r)*	volunteer	*Freiwillige(r)*	to confess	*gestehen*		

B   Read the text again and make a list of the following:

1   the withdrawal symptoms people felt   2   the things that some people started to do again

4   GETTING IT RIGHT   → Simple past, SB S. 251

Put the underlined verbs into the simple past. Use the list of irregular verbs on page 357 of the student's book to help you.

SARAH GETS A SHOCK

Sarah goes _____¹ online, opens _____² her Facebook account and checks _____³ her messages. She finds _____⁴ one with a picture of herself at a party and is _____⁵ shocked. At first, she thinks _____⁶ there is _____⁷ only one message, but then she finds _____⁸ another and another. She doesn't _____⁹ know what to do.

At school, she sits _____¹⁰ in the classroom and looks _____¹¹ around her. Are _____¹² these people her friends or her enemies now? How much do _____¹³ they know about her? Sarah doesn't _____¹⁴ notice the teacher and can't _____¹⁵ answer his questions. The bell rings _____¹⁶ and the lesson is _____¹⁷ over. Sarah leaves _____¹⁸ the classroom and understands _____¹⁹ one thing: She must _____²⁰ tell someone, but who?

5 LISTENING

→ Rezeption: Hörverstehen, SB S. 225

A Listen to the phone call between Mrs Seale and the mother who brought her son to the party and say if the following statements are true or false. Correct the false statements.

1 Catherine Seale phones Margaret Green.
2 The two women's sons are in the same class at school.
3 Margaret Green knows that the Seales are on holiday in France.
4 Margaret Green is in the front garden of Catherine's house.
5 Christopher told his mother he planned to throw a party.
6 The party is out of control.
7 The riot police are trying to break into the house through the roof.
8 The riot police are blocking the street.
9 Catherine's son planned to pay a bouncer to make sure only the right guests got in.
10 Mrs Green stopped the people wrecking the front garden.

B Listen again and complete the sentences with the words you hear. They are also in the text on page 40 of the student's book.

Margaret	There are young people everywhere, some are drunk and _____¹ in the front garden.
Margaret	I think the boy on the roof is trying to open the _____².
Catherine	On my new carpet! They'll _____³ it!
Margaret	I would say hundreds. I'm so sorry to tell you all this but I think they must be _____⁴.
Margaret	I can't see him. He must be inside but I don't want to go in there with all those drunken _____⁵.
Catherine	My husband has been listening and we're getting the first _____⁶ back to London!

C Expand the notes below into Mrs Green's account of what she saw at the Seales' house.

> Margaret Green drove – Jamie – party – Christopher Seale's house
> When – (arrive) she (see) hundreds of young people – street – front garden
> The music – (be) extremely loud
> Jamie – (get) out – car – (walk) – house – (ring) – doorbell – (wait)
> Nobody – (open) – door – (push) – open – (go) inside
> When – door (open) – Mrs Green (see) – dancing – shouting
> Suddenly – (hear) – crash
> It – (come) – roof
> She – (look) up – (see) – teenager – roof
> The next thing – (see) – riot police
> They – (jump) out of – vans – (start) – break up – outside the house
> Mrs Green – (realise) – things – (be) out of control – (phoned) – Catherine Seale
> She – (think) – the Seales – (be) out for the evening
> She – (not know) – they (be) – holiday – France

6 GETTING IT RIGHT

→ Simple past ▪ Present perfect, SB S. 254

Complete the sentences with the simple past or the present perfect.

1 Sarah (not use) _____ Facebook for over twelve months now.

2 She last (use) _____ it last year.

3 Since then she (change) _____¹ schools and (make) _____² new friends.

4 The first few weeks at her new school (not be) _____¹ easy but after a month or so she (feel) _____² at home.

5 When she (tell) _____¹ her new friends about the cyberbullying, they (be) _____² shocked.

6 In the past, Sarah (spend) _____ at least three hours a day online.

7 This year she (not be) _____ online at all.

8 Her life (change) _____ a lot since she started at her new school.

9 So far this year she (start) _____¹ to play the piano and (do) _____² a lot more sport.

10 Last week her piano teacher (tell) _____¹ her she (play) _____² well for a beginner.

TECHNICAL OPTIONS

A Look at the text on page 44 of the student's book and then match the definitions a–j to the words 1–12. There are two words that do not have definitions. Write your own definitions for them.

1	algorithm	**a**	allow another person / other people to use or have something
2	to decrypt	**b**	formula that allows somebody to read a piece of information
3	to encrypt	**c**	not the same as any others
4	to intercept	**d**	open to people in general
5	key	**e**	person who receives something
6	message	**f**	piece of information that one person sends to another
7	public	**g**	put data into a form that other people cannot read
8	recipient	**h**	safe, protected
9	secret	**i**	set of mathematical instructions which you follow to do a calculation
10	secure	**j**	stop and take something that is going from one place to another before
11	to share sth		it gets there
12	unique		

B Use words from part A and other information from the text on page 44 of the student's book to explain what is happening in the diagram on the right.

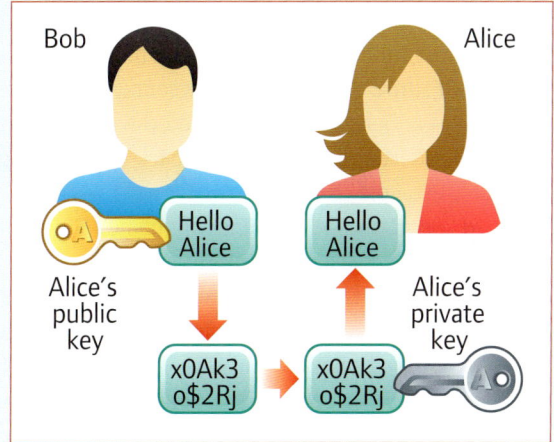

1 LOOKING AT THE TEXT

→ Rezeption: Leseverstehen, SB S. 214

A Look at text A on page 46 of the student's book and then match the sentence halves.

1	VW found that traditional advertising methods	a	use the stairs instead of the escalator.
2	In order to advertise their cars	b	clever, environmentally-friendly technology.
3	VW and their ad agency DDB therefore	c	in Stockholm, Sweden.
4	They started the campaign at a subway station	d	they realised they could play music with them.
5	They wanted to encourage people to	e	were becoming less and less effective.
6	VW made it attractive to use the stairs by	f	it went viral.
7	A lot of commuters chose to use the stairs when	g	VW needed to do something very different.
8	When VW released a video of the musical stairs	h	the public to enter a video competition.
9	After releasing two more viral videos, VW invited	i	invented the 'Fun Theory'.
10	The public now associate VW's cars with	j	making them produce notes like a piano.

B Now read texts B and C on pages 46 and 47 of the student's book and say if the statements are true (T) or false (F). Correct the false statements.

1 Very few people recycle things in Sweden. ☐

2 The bottle bank arcade pays people to recycle their glass. ☐

3 The bottle bank arcade communicates with the public. ☐

4 It is just as successful as a conventional bottle bank. ☐

5 VW and DDB want people to throw more rubbish into rubbish bins. ☐

6 VW and DDB's rubbish bin is always over a deep hole. ☐

7 When you throw something in, you hear a loud noise. ☐

8 The new bin has a maximum capacity of 72kg of rubbish per day. ☐

2 BUILDING SKILLS

→ Präsentieren, SB S. 243

Sevda and Frank have prepared a presentation on a fun solution to encourage people to wear safety belts in cars. However, their notes have got mixed up.

A Look at the *Useful phrases* on page 48 of the student's book and then put the presentation in the right order.

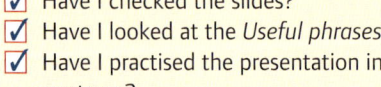

SKILLS CHECKLIST: Presentations

- ☑ Have I checked the slides?
- ☑ Have I looked at the *Useful phrases*?
- ☑ Have I practised the presentation in my team?

☐ **a Frank:** If you have any questions, we'll be pleased to answer them.

☐ **b Sevda:** As you can see from this slide, the dummies are injured because they are not wearing seat belts.

☐ **c Frank:** So how can we encourage people to wear seat belts? In this slide you can see an in-car entertainment screen for back seat passengers, for example children.

☐ **d Sevda:** Good morning. My name's Sevda and this is my colleague Frank.

☐ **e Frank:** Thanks for coming to this presentation.

☐ **f Sevda:** Today we're going to look at the problem of road safety.

☐ **g Frank:** To sum up, this solution makes it fun to be safe.

☐ **h Sevda:** In this slide you can see how a car and the passengers look after a car crash. By the way, this one has dummies, not real passengers.

☐ **i** **Sevda:** Let's begin by seeing what happens when a car crashes.
☐ **j** **Sevda:** Frank is now going to talk about a fun solution to make people wear seat belts.
☐ **k** **Frank:** But it only works if you're wearing your seat belt.
☐ **l** **Frank:** Children in the back seat naturally want to use the entertainment system.

B Practise giving the presentation with a partner.

3 **LISTENING**   → Rezeption: Hörverstehen, SB S. 225

A Look at your answers to exercise 7A on page 49 of the student's book to make sure you understand what the 4 Ps in the marketing mix are and then write them in column A of the table below.

B Listen to the recording and write down the information you hear to explain what each P refers to in this situation.

A Definition	B Description
_____	_____
_____	_____
_____	_____
_____	_____

4 **GETTING IT RIGHT**   → *Will* future ▪ *Going to* future, SB S. 257

A Tom Slater at Ad-Agency Plus in Edinburgh is discussing the launch of a new range of MyStyle wearables. Use the notes to make sentences with the *will* future (predicted actions), the *going to* future (intended actions) or the present progressive (fixed arrangements).

1 I'm sure / wearables / be / great success / near future (prediction)

_____

2 We / launch / the whole range / in Edinburgh / Monday (fixed arrangement)

_____

3 Each member / my team / demonstrate / different sort of wearable (intended action)

_____

4 I / wear / waterproof Android watch (intended action)

_____

5 We / have / press conference / 9 am (fixed arrangement)

_____

6 We / believe / demand for wearables / double / next six months (prediction)

_____

B Tom and his team are presenting MyStyle wearables at a big consumer electronics store in Edinburgh. Complete the sentences using the present progressive (fixed arrangements), the *going to* future (intended actions) or the *will* future (predicted actions).

Good morning and welcome to the launch of MyStyle's range of fantastic new wearables! This morning

_____[1] (introduce) you to a world of clever new products and

we're that sure that _____[2] (make) your life more fun! _____

_____³ (start) by showing you our Bodylife-tracker model. If you wear a Bodylife-tracker,

_____⁴ (be) able to record your physical, social and entertainment activities 24/7.

Top Olympic athlete Jessi Jones wore one for a whole week, and when you watch the video clip, _____

_____⁵ (see) how it works. We all know that Jessi _____⁶

(compete) for the UK in the World Championships next month. _____⁷ (take)

part in six events and we're certain that _____⁸ (win) six medals, so we at

MyStyle wish her good luck! After the video clip, _____⁹ (ask) you to fill in

postcards, so you can all take part in our 'Good Luck Jessi!' draw. We can tell you now that someone here

today _____¹⁰ (win) a free trip for two to the World Championships next month!

5 BUILDING SKILLS

→ Scannen nach Einzelinformationen im Text, SB S. 221

A Study the checklist and then scan the text and answer the questions.

1 When was Sony founded?
2 How many famous new products did Sony bring out bring out between 1955 and 2013?
3 What went wrong in 2011?

SKILLS CHECKLIST: Scanning
☑ Have I read the questions carefully?
☑ Have I focused on one type of information only?

SONY: The history of a household name

Ask anyone what they first think of when they hear the word 'Sony' and each generation will tell you something different. *Depending on* your age, you will say anything *ranging from* the transistor
5 radio (first made by Sony in 1955) to the Trinitron colour TV (1973), the Walkman (1979), the first CD player (1982), the camcorder (1987), the PlayStation (1994), AIBO the robotic dog (1999) or the first waterproof smartphone, tablet
10 computer and smartwatch (2013).

Sony started to think global as early as 1955 when the Tokyo Tsoshiu Kogyo company changed its brand name to Sony. Suddenly everyone was able to *pronounce* the Japanese company's name
15 and the Sony logo started to appear all over the world. In 1961 Sony was also the first Japanese company to sell its *shares* in the US, thereby opening the door to the world's biggest consumer market and preparing the ground for new
20 products.

Since being established by Akio Morita and Masaru Ibuka on 7 May 1946, Sony has consistently changed our lifestyles. Radios used to be large pieces of furniture made of wood which
25 people listened to at home. This changed in 1958 when Sony brought out the legendary portable TR-63 shirt pocket transistor radio described as 'the smallest transistor radio in the world'. People could suddenly listen to the radio anywhere they

chose. Up to the end of the 1970s, listening to 30
music had also meant staying in one place because record players, tape recorders and *jukeboxes* were big and heavy. This changed when Sony's *founder*, Masaru Ibuka asked an audio engineer to make him a portable tape player, so he could listen to 35
opera on *long-haul flights* from Japan to the US. The first Walkman was born and Sony kept the name for its MiniDisc (1991), MP3 player (2003) and Android Walkman (2012).

However, it hasn't always been *plain sailing*. 40
Sony's PlayStation network was hacked in 2011 and personal details from 77 million accounts were *compromised*. The company also stopped selling laptops and PCs in 2014 because they were not making a profit.   (343 words) 45

Vocabulary notes

depending on	je nach	founder	Gründer
ranging from … to	von … über … bis	long-haul flight	Langstreckenflug
to pronounce	aussprechen	plain sailing	einfach, problemlos
shares	Aktien	compromised	kompromittiert, nicht mehr sicher
jukebox	Musikbox		

B Match the paragraphs with these headings.

Major setbacks ▪ Famous inventions ▪ World market ▪ Mobile entertainment

C Answer the questions on the text in your own words as far as possible.

1 What two important things happened in 1955?
2 Why was it important for Sony to sell its shares in the US?
3 How did two of Sony's inventions change people's lifestyles?
4 Which market has Sony recently withdrawn from?

6 BUILDING SKILLS

→ Produktion: Schaubilder beschreiben und analysieren, SB S. 238

Look at the *Building skills* and *Useful phrases* boxes on pages 52 and 53 of the student's book and then complete the sentences about the graph on page 52. Use the simple present, the present perfect or the simple past.

The graph _____¹ (give) us a clear indication of how media ad spending in the US _____

_____² (increase) every year since 2011. It _____³ (rise) fastest in 2012 but then

_____⁴ (go) up more slowly in 2013. In general, the graph _____⁵ (show) us how,

over the years, spending _____⁶ (rise) by hundreds of millions of dollars every year.

The overall trend _____⁷ (be) still upwards, so we can say that American admen still

_____⁸ (not stop) investing large sums of money in media advertising.

Read the text on page 54 of the student's book again, then decide whether the statements below are true (T), false (F), or whether the information is not mentioned in the text (N). Correct the false statements.

TECHNICAL
OPTIONS

1 Beacons do not need a lot of energy to operate. ☐

2 Beacons will only send customers messages once they have entered the store. ☐

3 Smart phone users are worried that they will get a lot of unwanted messages every time they go shopping. ☐

4 Customers have to accept the messages even if they are not interested in them. ☐

5 Customers have to download special software to their phones in order to receive special deals. ☐

6 All customers will see the same beacon messages on their phones as they walk around the store. ☐

7 The beacon sends marketing information to the customer's phone. ☐

8 Apple was one of the first companies to use beacons in its stores. ☐

9 It is only possible to use Near Field Communication (NFC) in the Apple stores if you have an Apple account. ☐

7 Family and beyond

1 WORKING WITH WORDS

A Match these words from the text on pages 56 and 57 of the student's book to their opposites (1–8).

> borrow ■ criticize ■ extended ■ forget ■ huge ■ long-distance ■ noisy ■ together

1 lend _____

2 local _____

3 nuclear _____

4 praise _____

5 quiet _____

6 remember _____

7 separately _____

8 tiny _____

B Use pairs of words from part A to complete the following sentences.

1 My grandmother lives nearby in the _____¹ area but my aunt lives in Australia – that means spending a lot of money on _____² calls!

2 It's too _____¹ to talk properly here with all the children running around. But it's _____² outside, so let's go out there.

3 **A** Did you _____¹ to send Grandad's birthday card on the way home?

B Oh, no, I'm sorry, I _____². I'll go to the post office now.

4 **A** Are you and your parents going to travel _____¹?

B No, we're going _____². They're going by train, and I'm flying.

5 Traditionally, people used to live together as part of a large, _____¹ family, but in the modern world, the small, _____² family unit has become much more common.

6 We'd need a _____¹ house if the whole family lived together. There isn't enough room for our grandparents in this _____² house!

7 **A** Could I _____¹ some money for a few days?

B Well, I can _____² you €50 until Friday, but I'd have to have it back by then.

8 Why do you always _____¹ the children's school work so much? You need to be more positive and _____² them when they get things right.

2 GETTING IT RIGHT

→ Relative clauses, SB S. 269

A Complete the story with the statements in the box. Change them into relative clauses, using *who* or *which*.

> ■ They were offered jobs.
> ■ It paid very little.
> ■ He was hiring workers for a UK textile company.
> ■ He never gave up on anything.
> ■ It was very poor.
> ■ He came to England first.
> ■ They followed their arrival.
> ■ It would offer a better future.

Rajeev's Grandad Deepak was the one _____¹.

He and his young wife Mira came from a rural village in northern India _____

_____². They both had jobs at a local textile workshop _____

_____³. Not surprisingly, they wanted a new life – a life _____

_____ **4**. Then one day the village was visited by an agent

_____ **5**. Deepak and three other men

_____ **6** travelled together to Bradford in the

north of England. The months _____ **7** were

very difficult, but Deepak was a young man _____ **8**.

He worked and saved hard and six months later he was able to bring Mira over from India to join him.

B Now complete the dialogue with the statements in the box. Change them into relative clauses, leaving out *who* (or *that*) and *which* (or *that*) where possible.

- I've been most worried about them.
- I had to go next.
- She knew she might soon lose it.
- She pushed for us to move here.
- The company had already got rid of them.
- It was doing badly.
- It made us decide to move.
- The EU financial crisis hit it very badly.

One day, Lisa's dad was talking to Tom, a colleague at work.

Tom So tell me, what brought you over to England?

Dad Well, the thing _____

_____ **1** was work. You see, my wife

Kim had a job _____

_____ **2**. As for me, I worked

in Sales for a company _____

_____ **3**. There were others

_____ **4**, and I knew that I might be the one

_____ **5**.

Tom That must have been a very hard time. Ireland was one of the countries _____

_____ **6**, wasn't it?

Dad That's right, but I kept hoping our problems would go away. In the end, it was Kim

_____ **7**.

Tom Are you happy you made the move?

Dad I am now, but it's been hard. It's our children Lisa and Sam _____

_____ **8**. Especially Lisa. She tries to be cheerful, but I know she's often been

lonely. We're all looking forward to seeing all our family again over Christmas.

3 **WRITING AN INFORMAL LETTER**

Put the letter parts and sentences in order to write Lisa's letter.

Letter parts
Dublin 22   Lots of Love   29th May, 20..   53 West Road
Lisa   Dear Grandma and Grandpa   Ireland

Sentences
I'll be able to show you them when we get home for Christmas next month.
Well, I must stop now and run to catch the post.
This is to say a big 'thank you' for the money you kindly sent me for my birthday.
I can't wait for that because I miss you and all the family so much.
Thank you again!   So do Mum, Dad and Sam.
I'm going to put it towards some beautiful shoes I really, really want!

4 WORKING WITH WORDS

A Choose the correct preposition of place. There might be more than one correct answer.

1 He was going through the bin _____ (in / at) my bedroom.

2 I had a part-time job _____ (at / in) the little supermarket along the road.

3 I wanted to meet my friends _____ (in / at) town.

4 My grades were dropping because of stress _____ (in / at) home.

B Look at the map and complete the description with these prepositions of place.

> above ▪ across ▪ around ▪ at ▪ behind ▪ below ▪ between ▪ beyond ▪
> in ▪ in front of ▪ near ▪ next to ▪ on ▪ opposite

Carrie used to live _____ ¹ Number 7, Bow Road, very _____ ² the turn into Green
Street. Going right from there, you soon come to the bus stop _____ ³ the village green.
Then you come to the only shops in the village. Right _____ ⁴ the bus stop is the combined
post office and newspaper shop, and two doors farther along is the general village store.

_____ ⁵ them is the pub. The church and village hall are on the other side of the village
green, and _____ ⁶ the hall, there is a small playground for children. Just _____ ⁷
the church is the churchyard, and _____ ⁸ that and the hall is the village sports ground.

Coming back to the top of Bow Road, if you turn left there, the road soon divides into Sheep Street
and Park Road. Not far down Sheep Street, there is a path _____ ⁹ a steep hill to the right
of the road. That takes you up to the old castle _____ ¹⁰ the hill, high _____ ¹¹ the
village, with wonderful views _____ ¹² miles of open country. Back down at the end of
Sheep Street, you come to the Fish Hotel. Just _____ ¹³ the hotel is the River Wend, which
is famous for its fishing. _____ ¹⁴ the grounds of the hotel there is a sports centre, where
Carrie sometimes used to go to play tennis.

5 GETTING IT RIGHT

→ Simple past ▪ Past progressive, SB S. 251

Put the verbs in brackets in the simple past or past progressive.

Last year, three friends _____¹ (live) together in a student house. However, they

_____² (not get on) very well because no one _____³ (clean up)

after themselves. They _____⁴ (have) rules about the kitchen, but no one

_____⁵ (keep) to them. One evening they _____⁶ (all cook) at the

same time when they _____⁷ (have) a big argument. It _____⁸

(start) when Ellie _____⁹ (look for) a pan – but they _____¹⁰ (be)

all dirty. Tim _____¹¹ (try) to find some eggs, but when he _____¹²

(open) the fridge, he quickly _____¹³ (have to) shut it again because of the smell. Jamie

_____¹⁴ (look forward) to some soup, but when he _____¹⁵ (look)

in the cupboard it _____¹⁶ (be) all gone. At first they all _____¹⁷

(shout) at each other, but then they _____¹⁸ (agree) to change their ways.

6 BUILDING SKILLS

→ Rezeption: Hörverstehen, SB S. 225

Listen to Carrie's interview with the benefits officer and complete his notes.

7

PERSONAL DETAILS

Family name: _____¹   First name(s): _____²

Age: _____³   Date of birth: _____⁴

Address: _____⁵

Post code: _____⁶   Telephone (mobile): _____⁷

A Use verbs from the word snake to complete the advertisement for Robo-Servant below. There is one verb more than you need.

B Imagine you have a domestic robot like Robo-Servant at home. Use expressions from part A and your own ideas to write your robot's 'diary' for one day.

TECHNICAL OPTIONS

ACQUIREANSWERCLEANCLEANDOFEEDFETCHLOADOPERATEPERFORMPICKWATER

ROBO-SERVANT will …

_____¹ your floors – no more embarrassing dirty floors when guests arrive!

_____² your plants, so that they don't die when you forget about them.

_____³ your pets when you go away on holiday.

_____⁴ things from the fridge while you watch TV.

_____⁵ the microwave to cook your dinner.

_____⁶ the dishwasher with your dirty dishes.

_____⁷ the door when your friends arrive.

_____⁸ up toys when the kids have finished playing.

_____⁹ the toilet – because nobody likes to do that job!

_____¹⁰ all of your laundry – you can just throw your dirty clothes on the floor!

Best of all, ROBO-SERVANT will _____¹¹ new capabilities according to the needs of your family.

1 LISTENING

→ Rezeption: Hörverstehen, SB S. 225

8 A careers advisor at the National Careers Service is helping two students to choose a suitable career. Listen to the two dialogues and fill in as much of the table as possible.

	Meera	Christopher
Age	_____ 1	_____ 8
Dream job	_____ 2	_____ 9
Free time activities	_____ 3	_____ 10
Favourite subject(s)	_____ 4	_____ 11
Least favourite subject(s)	_____ 5	_____ 12
Work experience	_____ 6	_____ 13
Recommendation	_____ 7	_____ 14

2 LOOKING AT THE TEXT

→ Rezeption: Leseverstehen, SB S. 214

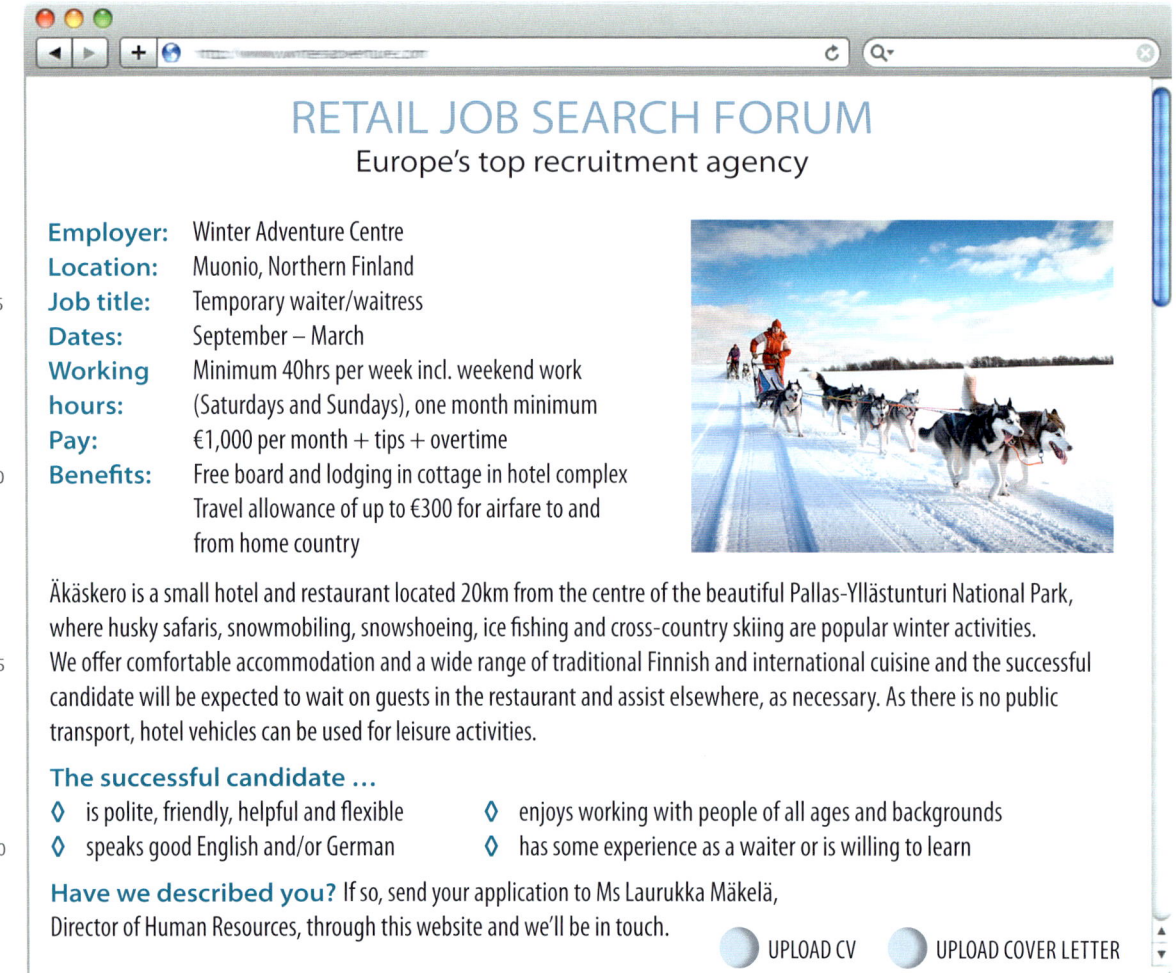

RETAIL JOB SEARCH FORUM
Europe's top recruitment agency

5

Employer: Winter Adventure Centre
Location: Muonio, Northern Finland
Job title: Temporary waiter/waitress
Dates: September – March
Working hours: Minimum 40hrs per week incl. weekend work (Saturdays and Sundays), one month minimum
Pay: €1,000 per month + tips + overtime

10 **Benefits:** Free board and lodging in cottage in hotel complex
Travel allowance of up to €300 for airfare to and from home country

Äkäskero is a small hotel and restaurant located 20km from the centre of the beautiful Pallas-Yllästunturi National Park, where husky safaris, snowmobiling, snowshoeing, ice fishing and cross-country skiing are popular winter activities.

15 We offer comfortable accommodation and a wide range of traditional Finnish and international cuisine and the successful candidate will be expected to wait on guests in the restaurant and assist elsewhere, as necessary. As there is no public transport, hotel vehicles can be used for leisure activities.

The successful candidate ...

20 ◊ is polite, friendly, helpful and flexible
◊ speaks good English and/or German
◊ enjoys working with people of all ages and backgrounds
◊ has some experience as a waiter or is willing to learn

Have we described you? If so, send your application to Ms Laurukka Mäkelä, Director of Human Resources, through this website and we'll be in touch.

UPLOAD CV   UPLOAD COVER LETTER

A Use the information in the advertisement to make notes on the following categories:

1	Length of contract	3	Accommodation	5	Insurance
2	Allowance	4	Food	6	Travel expenses

B Match the words in the box with the definitions below.

waiter/waitress ▪ tip ▪ located ▪ range ▪ leisure ▪ experience ▪ willing ▪ application

1 CV and cover letter
2 free time
3 knowledge or skill gained from doing something
4 money given for good service, e.g. in a restaurant or hotel

5 person who serves guests in a restaurant
6 prepared or ready to do something
7 situated
8 variety

3 BUILDING SKILLS

→ Schriftliche Mediation, SB S. 240

Sie sollen einen Blogbeitrag über „Ferienjobs im Ausland" für die Homepage Ihrer Schule schreiben. Lesen Sie zuerst die *Skills checklist* über schriftliche Mediation durch, und schreiben Sie dann einen Beitrag, in dem Sie die wichtigsten Vor- und Nachteile des Jobs am *Winter Adventure Centre* in Finnland (Übung 2) beschreiben. Erklären Sie auch, ob Sie die Stelle empfehlen würden oder nicht.

SKILLS CHECKLIST: Written mediation

☑ Have I read the situation and instructions carefully?
☑ Have I read through the text and marked relevant information?
☑ Have I written the right sort of text?

4 WORKING WITH WORDS

Use words from the box to complete the letter from a company director to his employees explaining why they now need to hot-desk.

by default ▪ challenge ▪ downsize ▪ dress down ▪ filing cabinet ▪ gradual ▪ Human Resources ▪ property ▪ requires ▪ workforce

Dear colleagues,

I am sure you have all noticed the _____¹ changes that are happening around us. Five years ago we had a _____² of 350. Now the total number of employees is 575. In simple terms, our company is becoming too big for the building we are in.

So what can we do to deal with this _____³? One answer would be to _____⁴ the company, but making it smaller would mean job losses. Another would be to look for a bigger building, but the price of _____⁵ in our area is far too high.

Research has shown that not every employee _____⁶ a desk every day, and some desks are even empty four days a week. We therefore intend to introduce hot-desking, which is when every employee has a _____⁷ on wheels but no fixed desk. The new system will be demonstrated by the director of the _____⁸ department next Monday at 10 am. We hope you will attend this very important meeting and look forward to your co-operation.

Wallace Baxter
Managing Director

5 **GETTING IT RIGHT** → *If* sentences, SB S. 264

A Use the right form of the verbs in brackets (*if* sentences type 1) to complete the dialogue between a student and his mother.

Mother Have you seen this brochure about jobs, Nicholas? It says you _____¹ (not have) much chance of finding a good job if you _____² (not apply) early.

Student But not this early! If I _____³ (send) an employer an application now, they _____ _____⁴ (tell) me to apply next year.

Mother But if you _____⁵ (contact) them this year, they _____⁶ (put) you on their waiting list, Nicholas! What's wrong with that?

Student It's stupid. If I _____⁷ (change) my mind, I _____⁸ (be) on the wrong waiting list.

Mother Well, I know from experience that you _____⁹ (not find) anything if you _____¹⁰ (wait) too long.

B Use the right form of the verbs in brackets (*if* sentences type 2) to complete the telephone conversation between Angela Jolly, a secretary at ICL computer services, and her friend Ramona, who is a school secretary.

Ramona Hi Angie! How are things?

Angela Could be better. I think I _____¹ (be) a lot happier if I _____² (have) a job like yours.

Ramona Well, if you _____³ (work) here, you _____⁴ (deal) with hundreds of people every week. Sometimes it's very stressful.

Angela Well, I'm at home alone all day working on the phone and the computer. It _____⁵ (be) wonderful if I _____⁶ (see) people every day! I think I _____ _____⁷ (accept) a pay cut if it _____⁸ (mean) seeing more people again.

Ramona I see what you mean. _____⁹ (you / take) a part-time job at a school if one _____¹⁰ (come) up? I could do with some help here.

Angela Yes! That sounds absolutely marvellous!

6 **BUILDING SKILLS** → Produktion: Eine Stellungnahme schreiben, S. 234

A Use the expressions in the box to fill in the gaps in the comment about young people moving away from home for work. You can look at the *Language for writing* on the back flap of the student's book if you need help.

another point to consider is this ▪ as a consequence ▪
firstly ▪ in my opinion ▪ to conclude ▪
on the other hand ▪ on the whole ▪ secondly ▪
there are several questions to think about
when discussing ▪ on the one hand

SKILLS CHECKLIST: Writing a comment

☑ Have I read the statement carefully und understood it?
☑ Have I structured my arguments logically, e.g. with a mind map or under headings?
☑ Have I included arguments for and against?
☑ Have I referred to the topic in my first sentence and stated my opinion in the conclusion?

1

the problems faced by young people when they move away from home. The first question is, how much do they really need their family, and the second is, what must they do to become truly independent?

_____ ², the family should give maximum support to a young person starting their first real job after school or college, _____ ³, because it is a very important moment in their life, _____ ⁴, because they may face big problems they can't solve alone and finally, because friends come and go but families are for life.

_____ ⁵ is it realistic in today's modern world to expect to find a job close to where you grew up and went to school? _____ ⁶ parents expect their children to be nearby to help them in their old age, but _____ ⁷ they want them to be independent, which often means being prepared to live and work a long way from home. _____ ⁸, the young person can easily feel guilty whatever they do.

_____ ⁹, I believe it's better to give young people the freedom to do what they want and be ready to help when things go wrong. _____ ¹⁰, I would say that help from the family is important at the beginning but less so as the young person becomes more and more independent.

B **Study the *Skills checklist* then write a comment expressing your personal opinion about the following statement: 'People who work long hours and never take a break just make other people suffer. Work isn't the only thing in life.'**

Read the text about training in Germany and then complete it with the sentences a–f below. There is one sentence that you do not need.

TECHNICAL OPTIONS

a However, in other countries this tradition may not exist.
b This way, it provides industry with skilled young workers with real-life training.
c One reason is that Germany has very low youth unemployment compared to many countries.
d Otherwise it is unlikely that importing German training methods will be successful.
e Some US states are adopting a German model, too.
f On the one hand, what students learn at school must complement what they learn in the company.

TRAINING THE GERMAN WAY

The German dual system combines theoretical training in vocational schools with practical in-company experience. ☐ ¹ Equally important, it makes it easier for young people to move from the world of school to the world of work. The success of the German dual training system depends on a close cooperation between educational institutions and companies that provide training. ☐ ² On the other hand, it shouldn't be so reduced that it is only relevant to that one job in that one company.

European countries such as Spain, Portugal, Italy, Greece, Latvia and Slovakia are looking at Germany's dual system. Beyond the borders of Europe, China, India, Vietnam and Russia are already working with the German government to change the way they train their young technicians. ☐ ³ Often it is local subsidiaries of German companies which lead the way.

However, the objective is not for these countries to *adopt* the German system completely, but to *adapt* parts of it to their own situation. Countries must take their own existing framework and conditions into consideration. ☐ ⁴ For example, in Germany there are many small and medium-sized companies that are training providers, and they are used to working closely with colleges, schools and universities. ☐ ⁵ In the US, for example, students often get their theoretical training first, and then after three years on a degree course, they are expected to go out and find a job. (228 words)

1 BUILDING SKILLS

→ Gründliches Lesen, SB S. 223

A Read the questions and underline words that may help you to find the relevant areas of the text.

1 What sort of ethnic community did Benjamin Zephaniah grow up in?
2 What went wrong with his education?
3 What did the BBC poll show?
4 Why might we be surprised by this?
5 Why did he refuse the offer of the OBE?

SKILLS CHECKLIST:
Reading for understanding

☑ Have I looked for key words in the questions?
☑ Have I found the key words in the text?
☑ Have I compared my answers with the questions and the text?

B Read the text and underline key words that help to provide the answers.

BENJAMIN OBADIAH IQBAL ZEPHANIAH:

British poet, story-teller and song-writer

Born in Britain in 1958. His parents were both from the Caribbean islands, and he grew up in Handsworth, Birmingham – an area he calls 'the Jamaican capital of Europe'. He left school at 13, unable to read or write. But with Jamaican music and poetry in his blood and angry street politics on his mind, he had a lot to say. He said it through public
5 performances of his hard-hitting poems. By the age of 15, he had *made a big name for himself* across Handsworth's large Jamaican and wider Afro-Caribbean community.

He did not fit well into the British social structure, and as a young man he was in trouble with the law and spent time in *prison*. Nor did his *anti-Establishment* ideas fit well, and over the years, he has continued his attacks on the Establishment. He has attacked, for
10 example, the British legal system, the monarchy, the political system, unfair treatment of minority groups in society and past *wrongdoings* of the British Empire.

Despite all this, he has also become one of Britain's most popular writers, and in a BBC poll he was voted the UK's third most-loved poet. He is Professor of Creative Writing at Brunel University, and his work is widely *recognized*.
15 However, he remains happily on the outside of society looking in. In 2003, for example, the Government offered him a medal, which he would receive from the Queen at Buckingham Palace. The medal was the OBE (short for The Order of the British Empire). His reply was immediate and clear though: 'Benjamin Zephaniah OBE – no way *Mr Blair*[1], no way Mrs Queen. I am *profoundly* anti-Empire.'   (264 words)

[1] Tony Blair, Prime Minister from 1997 to 2007

Benjamin Zephaniah performing in London in 2010

Vocabulary notes

to make a name for yourself	*sich einen Namen machen*	wrongdoing	*Vergehen*
prison	*Gefängnis*	to recognize	*anerkennen*
anti-Establishment	*gegen das Establishment*	profoundly	*zutiefst*

C Write full answers to questions 1–5 in part A.

D Read your answers carefully and compare them to the questions to make sure that you have given the details required.

2 WORKING WITH WORDS

A Complete the table with words from the text in exercise 1.

Noun (person)	Noun (thing)	Noun (person)	Noun (thing)
performer	_____ [1]	politician	_____ [3]
poet	_____ / _____ [2]	singer	_____ [4]

B Use pairs of words from A to complete the following.

1 **A** Lucy is a good _____¹, and she plays the guitar well, too.

   B Yes, and did you know that she's recently started writing her own _____² as well.

2 **A** I don't like the way the _____³ are running this country!

   B Well, if you don't agree with them, you'll have to go into _____⁴ yourself and try to change things.

3 He is a great _____⁵, so the best way to experience his poetry is to go to one of his live _____⁶.

4 Benjamin Zephaniah has written a number of stories such as *Refugee Boy*, but he first became known as a _____⁷, and he is still most famous for his _____⁸, which are usually short, often angry, and often funny, too.

3 GETTING IT RIGHT

→ *If* sentences, SB S. 264

Form type 3 conditionals from the following sentence parts, adding words as necessary. Start each sentence with *if*.

GETTING BACK TO AUSTRALIA

When Tom Blake was young, his family visited Australia on holiday. He loved the country and as he grew up, he often wished he could go back and get to know it better. Years later, with unemployment very high in the UK as he left college, his thoughts turned to Australia again.

1 unemployment not be so high in Britain / Tom find work without much difficulty

   If unemployment had not been so high in Britain, Tom would have _____

_____

2 get job in UK / stay Britain quite happily

_____

3 things go well for him / not wonder about work in other countries

_____

4 never be to Australia / be certain never think about working somewhere so far away

_____

_____

5 not look for work there though / miss perfect job for him – as tour guide for visitors

_____

_____

6 not take tour group up Gold Coast / never meet perfect girl for him, and champion surfer Jenny never become the love of his life!

_____

_____

4 GETTING IT RIGHT

→ Past perfect ▪ Simple past, SB S. 256

Put the verbs in brackets into the simple past or past perfect.

After Alem's father (go) _____ ¹ back to East Africa, the authorities (give) _____ ²

the teenager a new life in England – just as his father (expect) _____ ³. Even though

Alem (never visit) _____ ⁴ England before, he soon (begin) _____ ⁵

to feel comfortable with his new family, school and friends. It (be) _____ ⁶ much more pleasant than

the dangers he (experience) _____ ⁷ at home in East Africa with his parents.

But then, one day, Alem (receive) _____ ⁸ a letter from his father with terrible news of

what (happen) _____ ⁹ to his mother. He (learn) _____ ¹⁰ that she

(disappear) _____ ¹¹ before his father's return from England. Then Alem (read)

_____ ¹² the thing that he (be) _____ ¹³ most afraid of: his father's letter

(explain) _____ ¹⁴ how he (finally find) _____ ¹⁵

her dead body near the border between Eritrea and Ethiopia.

5 LISTENING

→ Rezeption: Hörverstehen, SB S. 225

9

Listen and complete the table with the missing figures.

Source: *www.migrationpolicy.org*

Population of the USA from 1970–2012 (millions)			
Year	Total	*Immigrants	Percentage (approx)
1970	203.2	9.6	³
1980	226.5	¹	6
1990	248.7	19.8	⁴
2000	281.4	²	11
2012	313.7	40.8	⁵

6 BUILDING SKILLS

→ Produktion: Statistiken beschreiben und analysieren, SB S. 238

A **Study the table to complete the analysis by circling the right words in brackets.**

Population of the USA from 1870–1970 (millions)			
Year	Total	Immigrants	Percentage
1870	38.6	5.8	14.9
1890	63.0	9.7	15.4
1910	92.2	14.0	15.2
1930	123.2	14.4	11.7
1950	151.3	10.4	6.9
1970	203.2	9.6	4.8

SKILLS Checklist: Analysing figures

☑ Have I read the labels carefully?
☑ Have I understood the units that the figures are presented in?

Between 1870 and 1910, US immigrant numbers (rose / fell)¹ from (under / over)² six million to
(a little under / almost exactly)³ fourteen million. At one point, their numbers (reached / fell to)⁴
15.4% of the country's total population. However, from then until 1930, there was (little change /
no change)⁵ in the immigrant population, while at the same time the total US population continued to
(fall / increase)⁶ (rapidly / slowly)⁷ – from (around / exactly)⁸ 92 million in 1910 to (approximately /
exactly)⁹ 123 million in 1930. This meant that as a percentage of the total, the trend was (downwards /
upwards)¹⁰ – from 15.2% to just 11.7%. This (rise / fall)¹¹ continued until 1970, when immigrants
formed (less than / more than)¹² 5% of America's population.

B Use the table in exercise 5 to complete a further analysis. Add language offered in 6A.

After the long _____¹ in immigrant numbers as a percentage of the total population, the trend

turned _____² after 1970, and numbers _____³ _____⁴. So,

by 2012, the immigrant population was _____⁵ 40 million – _____⁶

13% of the total.

C Use the Internet to find the latest possible figures. Use them to continue the analysis. Begin like this:

Since 2012, the figures have risen again to levels that the country last saw over a century ago.
The latest statistics show that …

A Read the text and find the best place for each of the headings in the box. Two sections
do not have a heading: write your own headings for them.

TECHNICAL OPTIONS

> A familiar pattern ▪ A world leader in high-speed rail ▪ How it all
> began ▪ Risks, but rich rewards ▪ The secret of China's success

1 _____

Since 2000, China has made rapid progress in high-speed train technology and is now one of the most important manufacturers
of high-speed trains along with Germany and Japan. At the same time, it has built the world's largest high-speed rail network.

2 _____

5   This is only one of the advanced manufacturing industries in which China is beginning to lead the world. Others include
electronics (computers, laptops, mobile phones), renewable energy (solar panels, wind turbines) and heavy machinery.

3 _____

How have Chinese companies and research organizations attained these impressive achievements so quickly? It is fair to say
that technology transfer has played a large part. This is the process by which technology, knowledge, skills and manufacturing
10 techniques are transferred from one country or organization to another.

4 _____

In the case of high-speed rail, technology transfer began in 2004 when the Japanese company Kawasaki signed a contract
worth US$740 million with China's biggest train company, CSR. According to the terms of the contract, Kawasaki would help
CSR to manufacture high-speed trains in China and also teach Chinese engineers their techniques. In 2005, the German company
15 Siemens made a similar agreement with another Chinese train company, CNR, to build the first high-speed rail line in China.

5 _____

The process of technology transfer is not new. In fact Japan, Taiwan and South Korea started by making copies of high-tech
imported products and then went on to become centres of technical innovation themselves.

6 _____

20 The difference here is that the Chinese government has actively encouraged technology transfer. From 2006 to 2011, China
had an official policy of requiring technology transfer from foreign companies that wanted to compete for Chinese government
contracts. Although that policy no longer exists, there is still strong pressure on foreign companies to provide technology transfer.

7 _____

With a population of nearly 1.4 billion people, China is the world's biggest market, so the advantages of trade with China are
25 bigger than the risks for technology companies.

B Read the German words and then find English words in the text from part A with the same meanings.

1 Hochgeschwindigkeits-	3 Fertigung	5 Großgeräte	7 Vertrag
2 fortschrittlich	4 erneuerbar	6 Errungenschaft	8 konkurrieren

1 WORKING WITH WORDS

Complete the word families using forms from the five texts on page 90 of the student's book.

Verb	Noun	Noun (person)	Adjective
to produce	production	_____ 1	productive
_____	_____ 2	_____	charitable
_____ 3	donation	_____ 4	_____
to complain	_____ 5	_____	_____
to sponsor	_____ 6	sponsor	_____
_____	_____ 7	accountant	_____
_____ 8	empowerment	_____	_____
to amaze	amazement	_____	_____ 9
to save	_____ 10	_____	safe
_____	_____ 11	companion	_____
_____	homelessness	_____	_____ 12

2 BUILDING SKILLS

→ Produktion: Schaubilder beschreiben und analysieren, SB S. 238

Foreign aid

In 1970 the world's richest countries promised to increase their annual aid budgets to 0.7% of gross national income (GNI). GNI means a country's income generated both inside and outside the country.

SKILLS CHECKLIST: Comparing figures in charts

- ☑ Have I pointed out the most striking features?
- ☑ Have I contrasted categories with each other?
- ☑ Have I described the relationships between the categories?

A Study the chart and say ...

1 which country is closest to reaching the 0.7% target. _____

2 which country is furthest from the target.

_____

3 which countries donate almost the same proportion of their GNI. _____

_____

4 which English-speaking country donates the highest percentage of its GNI.

_____

5 which country is in sixth place in the chart.

_____

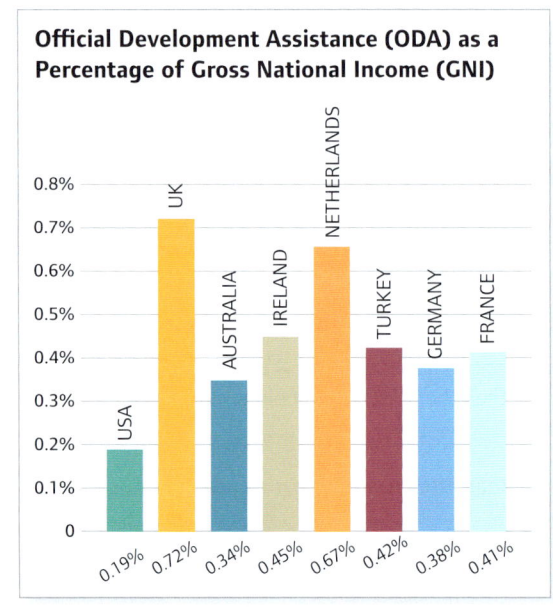

Official Development Assistance (ODA) as a Percentage of Gross National Income (GNI)

USA 0.19% · UK 0.72% · AUSTRALIA 0.34% · IRELAND 0.45% · NETHERLANDS 0.67% · TURKEY 0.42% · GERMANY 0.38% · FRANCE 0.41%

B Use expressions from the *Building skills* box on page 92 and the *Useful phrases* on page 93 of the student's book to complete the text.

The chart shows the _____¹ of their GNI that rich countries spend on aid, and we

can _____² see that there are big differences. The UK is in first _____³

while Germany only _____⁴ sixth, and the figure in the first _____⁵ shows

us that the USA is last. The _____⁶ for Germany (0.38%) is exactly _____⁷ as

much as for the USA (0.19%). Australia (0.34%) spends about _____⁸ as much on aid as the

Netherlands (0.67%).

C Study the chart about individual giving on page 92 of the student's book and compare it with this chart about government giving. Write 4–5 sentences to show the differences.

Begin like this: *Whereas private American individuals donate most money to help others, their government ...*

3 LOOKING AT THE TEXTS

→ Rezeption: Leseverstehen, SB S. 214

A Read the texts on page 94 of the student's book and say if the following statements are true (T), false (F) or not in the text (N). Correct the false statements.

1 Kevin and Sandra Forkan were in Sri Lanka with four of their children. ☐

2 The children who survived were near the British Embassy. ☐

3 The British Embassy gave them a lot of help. ☐

4 The Forkan children were strong because their parents taught them to think of themselves first. ☐

5 The two brothers learned a lot about business when they travelled the world separately. ☐

6 They founded a flip-flop company in India with Mahatma Gandhi. ☐

7 The Gandys Foundation is a company which makes flip-flops. ☐

8 Paul and Rob Forkan plan to open more than one children's home. ☐

B Can you find the words hidden in the anagrams below? The answers are all in the *Orphans for Orphans* text on page 94 of the student's book.

1 LNBIGSSI ☐☐☐☐☐☐☐☐

2 EAIDCV ☐☐☐☐☐☐

3 TIHKHEIDCH ☐☐☐☐☐☐☐☐☐☐

4 ETTGNRHS ☐☐☐☐☐☐☐☐

5 RTAAIHINNMAU ☐☐☐☐☐☐☐☐☐☐☐☐

6 SEAPAOHRGN ☐☐☐☐☐☐☐☐☐☐

7 RLIVUVAS ☐☐☐☐☐☐☐☐

8 IYRCHAT ☐☐☐☐☐☐☐

4 LISTENING

→ Rezeption: Hörverstehen, SB S. 225

Listen to the podcast about the work of *Rebuilding Sri Lanka*, a charity set up after the tsunami in 2004 and complete the sentences with a, b or c.

Vocabulary notes	
to borrow a book	*ein Buch ausleihen*
to lend a book	*jdm. ein Buch leihen*

1 The tsunami
  a destroyed Clare Allen's hotel.
  b didn't destroy Clare Allen's hotel.
  c killed Clare Allen's daughter.

2 After the tsunami
  a a million Sri Lankans were homeless.
  b a million Sri Lankans were left dead.
  c 40,000 Sri Lankans were homeless.

3 The *Rebuilding Sri Lanka* charity
  a plans to build five libraries.
  b is building five libraries.
  c has built five libraries.

4 Schoolchildren who wish to pass their school-leaving exams
  a can borrow books from the *Rebuilding Sri Lanka* charity's libraries.
  b receive £2,000 from the *Rebuilding Sri Lanka* charity.
  c receive extra lessons from the *Rebuilding Sri Lanka* charity.

5 The *Rebuilding Sri Lanka* charity has a library which
  a lends out 2,700 books every Saturday.
  b lends out more than 200 books every Saturday.
  c is closed to its 2,700 members on Saturday.

6 The *Rebuilding Sri Lanka* charity
  a provides schoolchildren with cheap meals at school.
  b encourages children to go to school by giving them free food.
  c teaches schoolchildren to cook their own food at school.

7 The *Rebuilding Sri Lanka* charity has a centre
  a for traumatized children.
  b for traumatized parents.
  c where counsellors can receive training.

8 Most of the money donated to the *Rebuilding Sri Lanka* charity is spent on
  a administration.
  b its website design.
  c people in need.

5 GETTING IT RIGHT

→ Present perfect ▪ Present perfect progressive, SB S. 253

A Write the present perfect forms of the verbs in the table.

Verb	Simple statement	Question	Negative
1 to ask (I)	I've ... ¹	Have I ... ²	³
2 to drive (you)	⁴	⁵	⁶
3 to fall (she)	⁷	⁸	⁹
4 to feel (we)	¹⁰	¹¹	¹²
5 to wear (they)	¹³	¹⁴	¹⁵

B Now write the present perfect progressive forms of the same verbs in the table.

Verb	Simple statement	Question	Negative
1 to ask (I)	_____ 1	_____ 2	_____ 3
2 to drive (you)	_____ 4	_____ 5	_____ 6
3 to fall (she)	_____ 7	_____ 8	_____ 9
4 to feel (we)	_____ 10	_____ 11	_____ 12
5 to wear (they)	_____ 13	_____ 14	_____ 15

C Complete the sentences with the present perfect or the present perfect progressive. Use the present perfect progressive when possible.

1 Rob and Paul Forkan _____ (write) a book called *Tsunami Kids*.

2 They _____ (sell) thousands of copies already.

3 The two brothers _____ (sell) Gandys flip-flops since 2012.

4 Katy Brown is a bookshop assistant and _____ (wear) her Gandys

for eight hours, since she started work this morning.

5 She _____ (buy) two pairs of Gandys flip-flops.

6 So far this year Katy _____ (donate) £25 to charity.

7 Her shop _____ (start) to collect money for good causes.

8 She _____ (work) at the shop for two months now.

9 She _____ (serve) customers since 9 o'clock this morning.

10 Nine customers _____ (buy) a copy of *Tsunami Kids* today.

Complete the crossword with the English translations of the German words. They are all in the text on page 98 of the student's book.

TECHNICAL OPTIONS

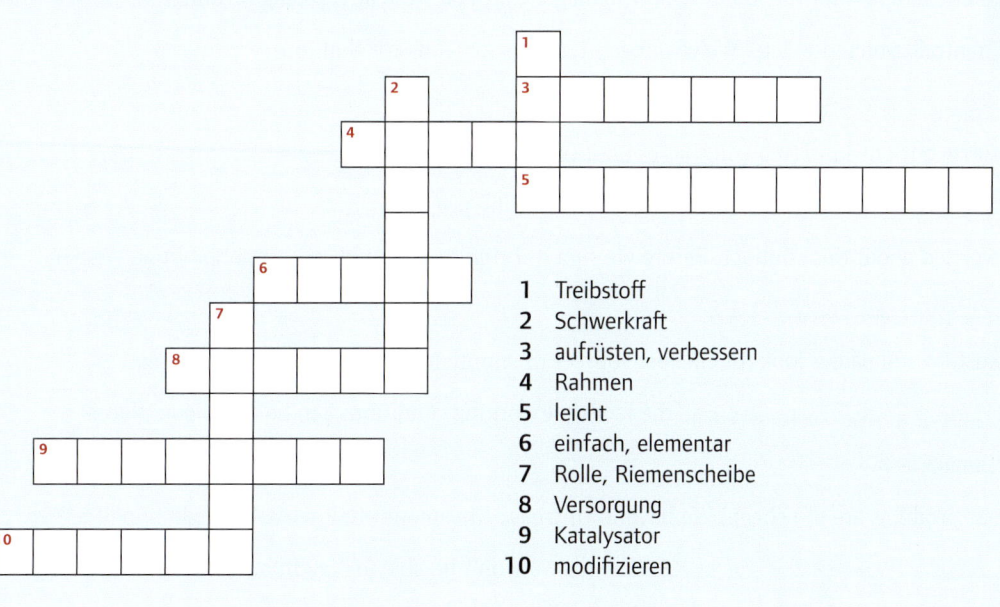

1 Treibstoff
2 Schwerkraft
3 aufrüsten, verbessern
4 Rahmen
5 leicht
6 einfach, elementar
7 Rolle, Riemenscheibe
8 Versorgung
9 Katalysator
10 modifizieren

1 WORKING WITH WORDS

A Match these nouns from the text on page 100 of the student's book to the verb-noun pairs below.

action • contact • a contract • an order • quality

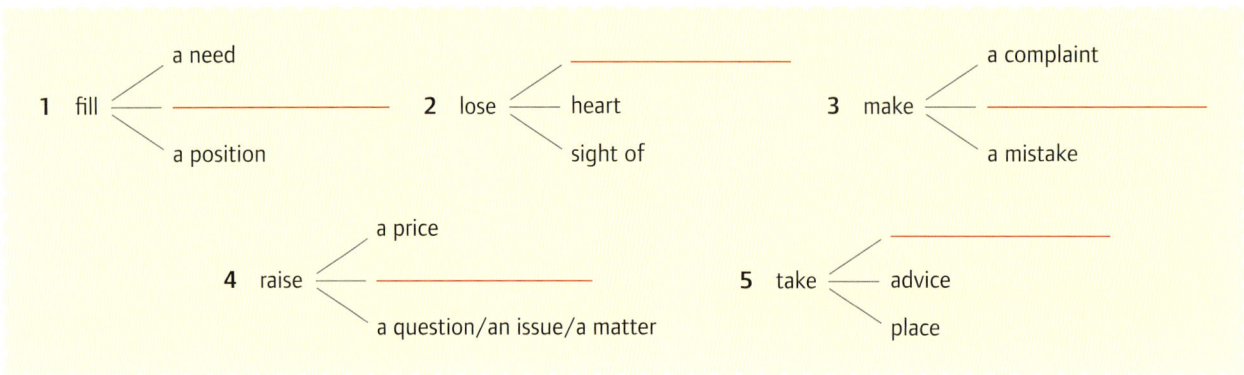

1 fill
— a need
— _____
— a position

2 lose
— _____
— heart
— sight of

3 make
— a complaint
— _____
— a mistake

4 raise
— a price
— _____
— a question/an issue/a matter

5 take
— _____
— advice
— place

B Replace the words in brackets with verb-noun pairs from part A. Make any changes necessary.

1 I think I've (got something wrong) _____ with these figures. They don't match the figures on the bill.

2 The Sunrise is a cheap, reliable car that (provides something necessary) _____ in the Indian market.

3 We've agreed that the next union meeting will (happen) _____ at 8 pm on Friday, 10 March.

4 When Tony became unemployed, he tried hard to find a new job, but slowly he (stopped hoping) _____ .

5 Before the company decides to build the new factory, I'd like to (ask something) _____ _____ about costs.

6 **A** I'd like to apply for the job of export manager that you were advertising recently.

 B I'm afraid you're too late. We've already (chosen someone for that job) _____ .

7 I'm sorry, but I need to (tell you that I'm not happy) _____ about the equipment that you sold us: it's not working properly.

8 I'm worried about this contract. Before we sign it, I think we should (ask somebody to advise us) _____ .

9 As western companies look for cheaper sources of supply in SE Asia, they often (forget) _____ the fact that working conditions can be terrible in places like Bangladesh.

10 All our products are too cheap! We have to (increase the amount that we ask people to pay us) _____ , or we won't be able to stay in business for much longer!

2 **GETTING IT RIGHT**

→ The passive, SB S. 261

A Use the simple present passive to describe a process. Add '*by + agent*' if necessary.

1 Farmers from all over the Gumutindo district grow coffee organically.

Coffee is _____

2 Then they bring the coffee to the new central production facility.

_____

3 There, highly-trained senior staff check quality and quantity.

_____

4 Then workers process the raw coffee in carefully-controlled conditions.

_____

5 After that, the Cooperative's new, automated equipment packs the coffee.

_____

6 Finally, they send the finished product to Mombasa for export to Europe and America.

_____

B Turn Steve Race's spoken comments into part of the journalist's formal report. Put the underlined comments into the correct passive tenses. Add '*by + agent*' if necessary.

So it's finally happened – and I'm angry. The company owners up in New York have closed the factory here in Virginia, and they've thrown 200 workers out of our jobs. I hear they made the decision last summer, but they didn't tell the workforce till last month. It seems they'll send all the equipment from the Virginia plant to a new factory in Indonesia, and people there will produce the same furniture for a quarter of the pay.

But when they move production offshore like this, it exports American jobs, too, and that damages the American economy. Don't these New York money men understand? It's crazy! If we close every US factory, we will completely destroy the US economy. Then who will buy all those 'made in Asia' products?

200 JOBS LOST AT ACE FURNITURE
The ACE FURNITURE factory here in Virginia

_____
_____
_____
_____
_____
_____
_____
_____
_____
_____
_____

3 BUILDING SKILLS

→ Produktion: Cartoons beschreiben und analysieren, SB S. 236

Follow these steps to write a cartoon analysis:

1 Describe the cartoon.
2 Explain this ironic comment on the effects of globalization.
3 Use the newspaper headlines to explain further.
4 Comment on the manager's words in the cartoon.
5 Say what the cartoonist is attacking here.

SKILLS CHECKLIST: Describing cartoons

☑ Have I read the caption(s) or speech bubble(s)?
☑ Have I described everything in the cartoon?
☑ Have I used the present progressive to describe what is happening?

DEVELOPED ECONOMIES
NOT COMPETITIVE
WITH FAR EAST

MANY US AND EUROPEAN JOBS
EXPORTED TO DEVELOPING WORLD

UNCERTAIN FUTURE
FOR WESTERN WORKERS

This cartoon shows _____
_____
_____

WE'RE GOING TO HAVE TO LET YOU GO...WE'VE FOUND SOMEONE
IN CHINA WHO IS 45% BETTER AT BEING YOU FOR 24% LESS

_____
_____
_____
_____

4 LISTENING

→ Rezeption: Hörverstehen, SB S. 225

A Listen to the Twin Trading field officer's report on Gumutindo Cooperative's coffee sales. Complete the column 'Changes in production'.

Period		Changes in production (kilos)	Description of changes
Year 1	1st half	0 – 500	rose gradually
	2nd half	_____ 1	_____ 8
Year 2	1st half	_____ 2	_____ 9
	2nd half	_____ 3	_____ 10
Year 3	1st half	_____ 4	_____ 11
	2nd half	_____ 5	_____ 12
Year 4	1st half	_____ 6	_____ 13
	2nd half	_____ 7	_____ 14

B Listen again, this time for the way the changes are described. Complete the column 'Description of changes'.

5 BUILDING SKILLS

→ Produktion: Schaubilder beschreiben und analysieren, SB S. 238

A Use the information from the table to complete the chart.

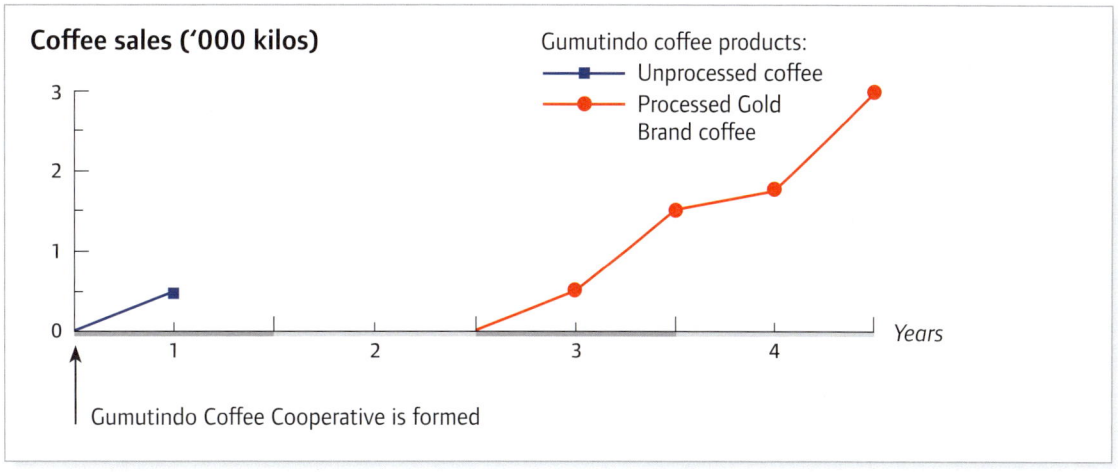

Coffee sales ('000 kilos)

Gumutindo coffee products:
- Unprocessed coffee
- Processed Gold Brand coffee

Years

Gumutindo Coffee Cooperative is formed

B Now describe sales of Gumutindo Gold Brand coffee. Start like this:

Gumutindo Gold Brand
In the first half of Year 3, sales _____ from _____ to ...

A Label the diagram using words from the box.

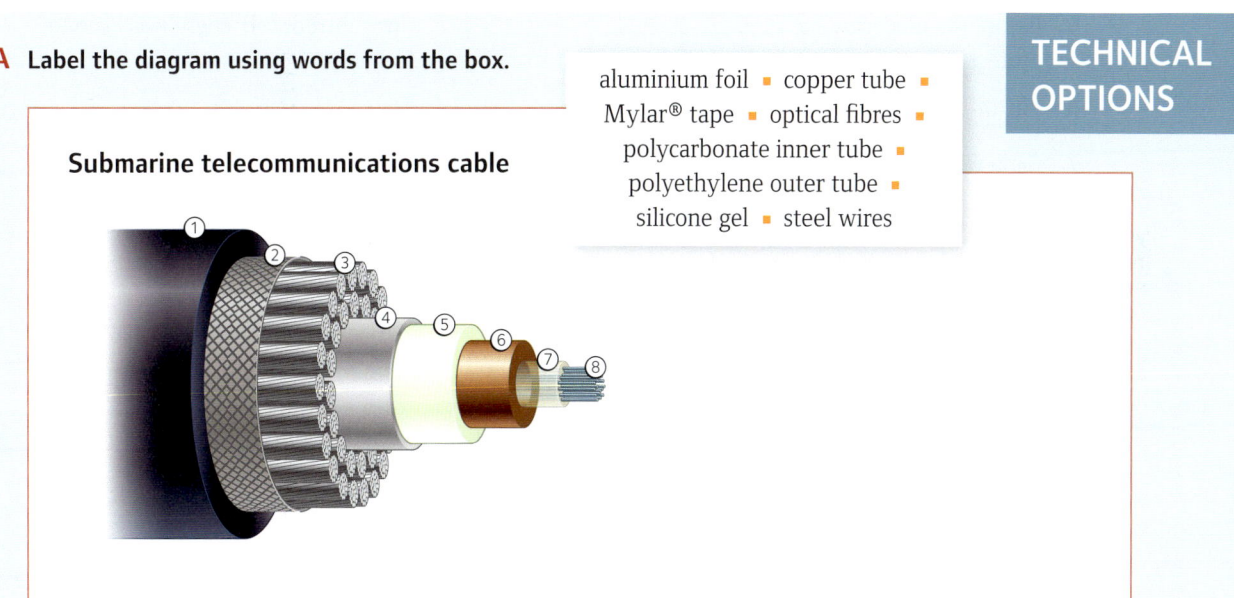

Submarine telecommunications cable

aluminium foil ▪ copper tube ▪
Mylar® tape ▪ optical fibres ▪
polycarbonate inner tube ▪
polyethylene outer tube ▪
silicone gel ▪ steel wires

B Match the descriptions to the labels from part A.

a Plastic layer that provides electrical insulation, separates the different metals and protects the inner cable from temperature changes.

b Strong, double layer of twisted metal wires that protects the cable from being stretched, squeezed or cut.

c Soft gel that protects optical fibres from stress and abrasion, does not dissolve in water.

d Thin layer of water-resistant metal to protect the inner cable from sea water which might penetrate the outer layers.

e Very thin but strong tube of woven plastic material that holds the steel wires in place.

f Thick flexible plastic outside layer to protect the cable from rocks etc. on the sea bed.

g Electrical conductor that provides high-voltage power to repeater stations along the cable.

h Very thin, long strands of glass or plastic that transmit data as light signals.

1 WORKING WITH WORDS

A Match words from box 1 with words from box 2 to form word pairs from the text on pages 110 and 111 of the student's book.

1
daytime ▪ entry-level ▪ job ▪ middle ▪ minimum ▪ pay ▪ production ▪ retail ▪ university ▪ welfare

2
application ▪ assistant ▪ degree ▪ industry ▪ job ▪ management ▪ packet ▪ system ▪ TV ▪ wage

B Use word pairs from A to complete the following sentences.

1 A lot of people don't earn enough to be able to support their families properly. The government

   needs to raise the _____ .

2 The _____ is very competitive. Look at the fierce competition
   between supermarkets, for example.

3 Tessa has always been interested in producing books and magazines, and now she's started work

   as a _____ with a big publisher.

4 Ralph was a junior manager for several years, but now he has risen to a job in _____

   _____ .

5 Before the modern _____ was introduced, there was little to
   protect the poor, the elderly and the sick, apart from family, friends and charity.

6 I'm applying for an _____ job, so it isn't very well paid, but it's a good start.

7 Carla will have to study for another four years if she wants to get a _____

   _____ .

8 It's very hard to find work at the moment. I've sent out hundreds of _____ ,
   but I've only been offered two interviews so far.

9 Tony isn't doing much about finding a job. He just sits at home and watches _____
   all day long!

10 I'm tired of being poor! It would be great if I could find a full-time job and get a proper _____

   _____ every month.

2 GETTING IT RIGHT

→ Modal verbs, SB S. 259

A Complete a reporter's interview with the publisher of the online publication *Business Now* by circling the right modal verbs in brackets.

Reporter Is it true that you don't usually pay your contributors?

Publisher That's right. In general, I find that we (needn't / mustn't)[1] pay because people want to give us their material anyway.

Reporter But is that right? It seems to me that you really (should / might)[2] pay. I mean, how (might / can)[3] writers go on writing if publishers don't pay them?

Publisher Well, most people who write for *Business Now* (can't / don't have to)[4] make money from it because they have other jobs.

Reporter	Yes, but your publication is a business like any other, and it seems to me that every business (must / may) [5] pay its suppliers properly – or else it isn't a real business.
Publisher	No, no, you (needn't / shouldn't) [6] think about it like that. You see, *Business Now* doesn't make big profits, so we simply (can't / mustn't) [7] pay much. And remember this, we (have to / may) [8] deal with many other costs, so free contributions help us to survive.
Reporter	So why do people do it?
Publisher	For various reasons, I think. For example, people (should / may) [9] write for *Business Now* because they want to share their ideas and help others in similar situations. There are others who (might / can't) [10] do it just to make a name for themselves in their own organizations.

B Complete the dialogues. Use *can/can't* or *could/couldn't* when possible. When necessary, use forms of *(not) be able to*.

1 **A** Have you prepared your new CV yet?

B I _____ [1] yet, but I _____ [2] have it ready by tomorrow.

2 **A** How did you get on at your interview?

B Well, I _____ [1] see that they were quite interested in me, but I

_____ [2] be sure that they were ready to offer me the job.

3 **A** What about the general test that the company asks all candidates to do? A lot of people

_____ [1] finish in the time that they allow.

B Yes, that went all right, I think, and I _____ [2] answer all the questions.

4 **A** Well done for getting the job! But I hear that they wanted you to start on Monday, so why aren't you at work now?

B I _____ [1] start straight away because I had to go away. But I told them and

luckily, I _____ [2] change the start date to next Monday.

---

3 **LISTENING**

→ Rezeption: Hörverstehen, SB S. 225

A Listen to Brazilian student Carlos use Skype to talk to someone at Windsor Park Retirement Home. Take notes about the resident for him.

> Name: _____ Age: _____ Years at WPRH: _____
> Family:
>   Wife: _____
>   Children/ages: _____
>   Grandchildren/ages: _____
> Interests: 1 _____ 2 _____ 3 _____

B Listen again and decide whether these statements are true (T) or false (F).

1 This is the first time that Carlos has talked to this elderly American. ☐

2 This person lived on his own for twelve years after his wife died. ☐

3 He moved to Windsor Park Retirement Home because he was lonely. ☐

4   His sons both have families, but not his daughter. ☐

5   His whole family gave him a surprise birthday party yesterday. ☐

6   They used the restaurant at Windsor Park. ☐

7   He enjoys various activities at Windsor Park, but he seems to enjoy going out even more. ☐

C **Now correct the false statements.**

_____

_____

_____

_____

4 GETTING IT RIGHT

→ The passive, SB S. 261

Rewrite the Mill Hill Retirement Home's rules more formally. Use passive modal forms.

RULES FOR VISITORS

1   Whenever possible, you should plan visits for normal visiting hours. (However, we may allow visits at other times by special arrangement.)

_____

_____

2   Please note that sometimes we may not allow a visit if a resident is very unwell.

_____

3   Visitors must sign in at reception.

_____

4   We are sorry, but you cannot bring pets into the building.

_____

5   You are welcome to eat with us, and you can order visitors' meals by phone or email 24 hours in advance.

_____

_____

6   All communication with staff is very welcome, but you should not interrupt nurses when preparing residents' medications.

_____

_____

5 BUILDING SKILLS

→ Ein Wörterbuch benutzen, SB S. 217

Read the dictionary definitions (1–6) and match them to sentences a–f below.

work /wɜːk/ verb [I or T]   **1** to do a job, especially the job you do to make money   **2** If a machine works, it operates correctly.   **3** If you work a machine, you make it operate.   **4** to be effective, to go according to plan   **5** to arrange for something to happen, especially by doing it secretly and cleverly   **6** to shape, change or process a substance

a My computer isn't working properly: things keep disappearing from the screen. _____

b Cut the pastry into circles and then work them into little cups to hold the mixture. _____

c I'm only working part-time at the moment, so I'm looking for a full-time job. _____

d I worked it so that Tom and Ann sat together at dinner and had a chance to talk. _____

e It'll take three people for us to be able to work this old machine properly. _____

f The medicine started to work almost immediately, and Sam soon began to feel better. _____

TECHNICAL OPTIONS

Read the text and then select suitable assistive technologies for the people described in sentences 1–4. Explain how each technology will help them.

1 David was paralyzed in a skiing accident. He is unable to move his arms and legs, but with help he is able to sit upright in a chair, he can speak and he can move his head from side to side.

2 Chloe has very poor eyesight. She can see light and dark, but she cannot read text on a screen unless it is very large. She can read Braille.

3 Margie is 85. She is quite active, but she has bad arthritis in her hands. She is also deaf.

4 Callum has cerebral palsy. He is unable to speak clearly and he has problems with fine motor skills – he finds it difficult to control the movement of his hands.

Assistive technology for computer users

Assistive technology helps people who have physical or cognitive disabilities and difficulties. Here are some examples.

Customized keyboards can help people who have motor skills problems or damaged hands. The keyboards may have keys that are larger or smaller than usual, or different arrangements of keys. Some are designed specially for use with one hand.

Electronic pointing devices allow computer users to control the cursor on the screen without using their hands.
5 The technologies to do this include ultrasound, infrared beams, eye movement tracking and devices that can read nerve signals or brain signals.

Sip-and-puff systems are activated by the user breathing in or out. They allow people who are paralyzed from the neck downwards to use a computer.

Joysticks and trackballs can be controlled by the user's hands, feet, chin, etc. They can be used to move the cursor
10 on the screen and select items. They are useful for people whose fingers are damaged by injury or arthritis.

Touch screens are familiar to most people now through their use in tablets and smartphones. They allow direct use of the computer by touching the screen. Desktop computer monitors can be adapted to use this technology, too. They are useful for people who do not have the fine motor skills to use a normal keyboard and mouse.

Light signals are useful when the user cannot hear computer sounds because of poor hearing, or is not directly in front
15 of the computer screen. They can be used to let the user know that an email has arrived or a computer command has been carried out.

On-screen keyboards are a feature of tablets and smart phones but can also be used with desktop computers. They show an image of a keyboard on the screen. This allows the user to select keys using a mouse, touch screen, trackball, joystick, switch or electronic pointing device. This is useful for people with damaged hands and mobility problems.

20 **Braille displays** can be read by blind people. They mechanically lift small round plastic or metal pins to form Braille characters so that the user can read the content of the screen.

Screen readers describe everything that is on the screen, including text, graphics, control buttons and menus. They are essential for blind internet users.

Speech recognition programs allow people to give commands and enter data by using their voices. They allow
25 people who are blind or paralyzed to use a computer. (407 words)

1 LOOKING AT THE TEXT

→ Grobverständnis, SB S. 214

A Skim the text quickly and decide which statement best describes what it is about.

- **a** Young Muslim girls from poor families are running away to the Middle East.
- **b** Young Muslim girls who run away feel that Western society doesn't value them.
- **c** Recent migrants are more in favour of terrorism.

UK MUSLIM COMMUNITY
DEVASTATED BY RUNAWAY JIHADI BRIDES

The press regularly write stories about young European men leaving to become foreign fighters in the Middle East and returning to Europe as hardened terrorists, but it took a little longer for society to realize that young girls were also leaving and rarely coming back. The UK's Muslim community is so *devastated* that in September 2014, Muslim women launched the 'Making A Stand' campaign to stop their children, in particular their daughters, running away and joining extremist groups in the Middle East.

In a moving letter to all young Muslim girls thinking of going out to join ISIS, they remind them that in the ISIS *caliphate*, girls should marry from the age of nine and women wear *veils* and are kept out of sight of society. They tell them that once in Syria or Iraq they will not be allowed to leave the caliphate and return to the UK, adding that many have tried but few have succeeded. They warn the young Muslim girls that they will have no chance to fulfil any dreams they may have about a better life and will lose their identity and freedom, because ISIS treats women as second-class citizens and not with the *dignity* and respect they are promised in Islam.

So what makes a young person decide to run away? A University of London study found that young Muslims *sympathizing* with terrorism were often born and brought up in the UK, had enough money but were socially isolated and suffered from depression. Recent migrants to the UK who came to the West to escape violence and war were found to be less ready to support radical ideas.

Another study found that Western society does not give young Muslims the feeling that they belong. Instead, they feel that society does not value them and in some cases places *restrictions* on how they can *practise* Islam, e.g. the burqa ban in France and Belgium. It describes how the leader of ISIS offers young women a new life in which they can help create a pure Islamic state with a variety of jobs and responsibilities for women, such as being a member of an all-women moral police force which makes sure that other women *keep* strictly *to* ISIS's interpretation of Sharia law. The study finishes by saying that the young women's reasons for joining the jihadis in the Middle East are not only political but also personal, with a strong element of naive romanticism. (408 words)

Vocabulary notes					
devastated	*am Boden zerstört*	dignity	*Würde*	to practise	*ausüben*
caliphate	*Kalifat*	to sympathize	*sympathisieren*	to keep to	*einhalten*
veil	*Schleier*	restriction	*Einschränkung*		

B Answer the questions about the text in exercise 1 in your own words as far as possible.

→ Umgang mit Operatoren, SB S. 232

1. Outline the problem that has shocked the UK's Muslim community.
2. Describe the action taken by the Muslim community to counteract this problem.
3. Contrast the life that a young Western woman can expect in the ISIS caliphate as described by its leader and by the members of *Making A Stand*.
4. Examine the factors which may make a young woman decide to become a jihadi bride.

2 WRITING

→ Eine Stellungnahme schreiben, SB S. 234

Write a comment on the topic of jihadi brides. Evaluate the explanations given in the text and comment on the roles played by the young women's friends, family, religious community and school.

3 WORKING WITH WORDS

A Complete the word families using forms from the text in exercise 1.

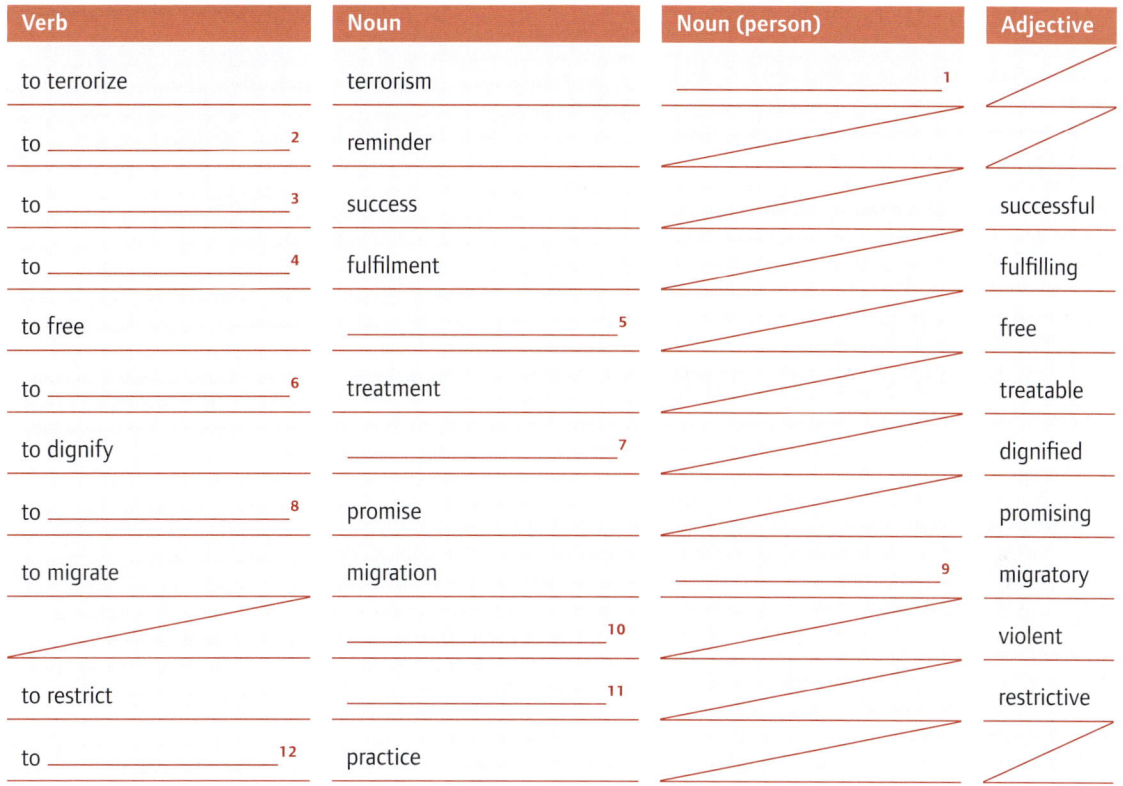

Verb	Noun	Noun (person)	Adjective
to terrorize	terrorism	_____ ¹	
to _____ ²	reminder		
to _____ ³	success		successful
to _____ ⁴	fulfilment		fulfilling
to free	_____ ⁵		free
to _____ ⁶	treatment		treatable
to dignify	_____ ⁷		dignified
to _____ ⁸	promise		promising
to migrate	migration	_____ ⁹	migratory
	_____ ¹⁰		violent
to restrict	_____ ¹¹		restrictive
to _____ ¹²	practice		

B Use ten of your answers in A to complete the text below. Make any necessary changes.

It is all too easy to see the young women who run away to _____ ¹ their dreams in Iraq
or Syria as dangerous _____ ² just like the armed Islamic fundamentalists we often see
on TV. It may seem strange but, just like other teenagers, they are simply rebelling and looking for their
_____ ³. They find that the _____ ⁴ placed on Islam by Western
society (e.g. the burqa ban) make it impossible for them to _____ ⁵ their religion in
the way they wish. They expect to be treated with _____ ⁶, but the mass media's
Islamophobia _____ ⁷ them every day that they do not belong. Some young Muslim
girls actually _____ ⁸ in reaching the caliphate and arrive expecting that the people
there will _____ ⁹ them with respect. Many are then shocked by the extreme
_____ ¹⁰ of the ISIS fighters, but by then it is too late to leave.

4 LISTENING

→ Rezeption: Hörverstehen, SB S. 225

13

Listen to the radio talk show about surveillance cameras and complete the sentences with a, b or c.

1 The policeman feels that surveillance cameras are
  a the best way of identifying people who break the law.
  b one of several ways of identifying people who break the law.
  c an unacceptable way of identifying people who break the law.

2 The journalist
  a totally agrees with the policeman.
  b totally disagrees with policeman.
  c agrees with some of what the policeman says.

3 The actor is willing to give up
 a some of his safety for the sake of privacy.
 b some of his privacy for the sake of safety.
 c neither his safety nor his privacy.

4 The student representative believes that
 a the world is a safer place now than in the past.
 b people have more privacy now than in the past.
 c surveillance cameras don't stop people breaking the law.

5 The student representative
 a believes the police are quite capable of breaking the law.
 b had her phone hacked by the police.
 c was injured by a mounted policeman at a demonstration.

6 The actor hit a photographer
 a in the street.
 b at a demonstration.
 c in a hospital.

5 GETTING IT RIGHT

→ Verb + infinitive ▪ Verb + gerund, SB S. 262

Choose an infinitive or gerund to complete these sentences. Sometimes there are two possible answers.

Digital dilemma

Banks encourage us (to open / opening)[1] an online account, shops want us (to download / downloading)[2] their app and more and more people are choosing (to shop / shopping)[3] online rather than in a crowded department store – but there's a downside. Opening any kind of digital account involves (to give / giving)[4] personal information to an organisation. Some people don't mind (to do / doing)[5] this and don't hesitate

5   (to provide / providing)[6] their bank account and credit card details. Experts therefore recommend (to use / using)[7] a different, strong password for each of our accounts and some even suggest (to change / changing)[8] these passwords every few months. This is where the digital dilemma begins. At first sight, a modern digital lifestyle seems (to be / being)[9] fast and convenient, and we like (to have / having)[10] more time for leisure activities. However, we can't afford (to lose / losing)[11] all our money to data thieves, so we constantly need

10   to change our passwords. One way to avoid (to have / having)[12] all this stress is to buy things in shops again and use paper for our bank transactions.

6 BUILDING SKILLS

→ Interaktion, SB S. 246

Use the expressions in the box to fill in the gaps in the discussion. You can look at the *Useful language* on the back flap of the student's book if you need help.

Do you see what I mean? ▪ I couldn't agree more! ▪ I see what you mean ▪
I'm afraid I can't accept ▪ I'm sorry to interrupt, but ▪ If you ask me ▪ Let me put it in another way ▪
So, is the basic idea that ▪ The main reason is ▪ There's some truth in what you say ▪
Well, as a matter of fact ▪ What's your view on

Listeners are phoning in to speak on the BBC radio talk show *World have your say*. The topic for discussion is surveillance cameras.

Talk show host … Just stay on the line for a moment will you, Ronald? Let's hear what our next caller thinks. It's Margaret in Ireland. Why do you think we need more surveillance cameras, Margaret?

Margaret _____[1], people are more out of control these days, especially young people, so we need cameras in schools as well.

Talk show host And why are they out of control, Margaret?

Margaret _____[2] that school doesn't give them enough to do, so they do stupid things in their free time.

Talk show host _____[3] surveillance cameras in schools, Ronald? Is it a place where young people have too much free time and are out of control?

Ronald	_____ 4! Margaret's exactly right! We should have cameras in schools.
Talk show host	We should have surveillance cameras in schools, say Margaret and Ronald. Our next caller is Noureddine in Morocco. Do you agree with Margaret and Ronald?
Noureddine	_____ 5, I don't. Schools are a place of learning where people must feel free. They shouldn't be a place where 'Big Brother is watching you', so _____ 6 the idea that we need to keep control of young people with surveillance cameras.
Talk show host	So what do you say to Noureddine about that, Margaret?
Margaret	_____ 7 because young people need *some* freedom. A school shouldn't be like a prison, so _____ _____ 8. But I do believe there isn't enough discipline. _____ _____ 9: Imagine if you sent your child to your local school and found out they were doing drugs at lunchtime. You'd be really worried, wouldn't you? So _____ 10? You think your children are learning what they need for life and all they're doing is learning to break the law!
Talk show host	_____ 11 if you give young people too much freedom, they'll break the law, Margaret? If you really believe that …
Noureddine	_____ 12 I think that what Margaret is suggesting is completely wrong …

Work out the anagrams to complete the text about space weather. The words are all from the unit.

SPACE WEATHER PROTECTION

Space weather is electromagnetic energy and SPETRACIL _____ 1 of matter that travel through space. It is a problem for astronauts, but on Earth our planet's atmosphere and GNAMECIT LIDEF

5 (2 words) _____ 2 protect us from it. However, there are two kinds of space weather that can affect us here on Earth. These are coronal mass ejections (CMEs) and solar flares.

A CME happens when the sun emits a huge ball

10 of plasma. It races out into space at 1.5–8 million kilometres an hour. When a CME hits the Earth's atmosphere, it can cause geomagnetic storms. Strong storms can knock out the entire TALLICREEC DIRG

(2 words) _____ 3: they can cause powerful STUNRERC _____ 4 15 in power lines and destroy MARNSTORSFER

_____ 5. A solar flare is a brief flash of electromagnetic radiation. It travels at the speed of light, so it can reach the Earth in minutes. It can GEDAMA _____ 6 or knock out satellites. 20

Fortunately, it is possible to protect ourselves against damaging space weather. Prediction helps us to protect BENUREVALL _____ 7 systems. We can already use satellites like NASA's Solar Dynamics Observatory to MOONIRT _____ 8, and 25 possibly forecast, solar flares and CMEs.   (183 words)

1 WORKING WITH WORDS

Each of the first sentences contains a word from pages 136 and 137 of the student's book in *italics*. Complete the second sentences with a word with a similar meaning from the box. Make any necessary changes.

> appear ▪ grow ▪ hugely ▪ lift ▪ opportunity ▪ reason for ▪ stop

1 Developing countries all aim to *raise* their levels of economic activity. By doing this, they can _____ their people out of poverty.

2 With China's rapid rise as a great economic power, its industries have developed *massively*. As we would expect, the country's energy needs have also increased _____ .

3 What's the *cause* of the increasing levels of CO_2 in the atmosphere? Most climate scientists agree that human activity is the main _____ this worrying change.

4 What happens if we can't *prevent* CO_2 levels from reaching 560ppm? If we don't _____ that from happening, most scientists say that disastrous climate changes will follow.

5 It's hard to be sure, but climate change *seems* to be happening already. For example, we _____ to get more wet weather in winter than we used to.

6 During the heaviest rains that have ever been recorded, the rivers *expanded* to twice their normal size last year. And the lakes _____ to three times their usual area.

7 The next international meeting on climate change offers another *chance* to control global CO_2 emissions. And that will give the world another _____ to limit climate change.

2 GETTING IT RIGHT

→ Indirect speech, SB S. 266

A **Report part of a debate on climate change. Use full forms of the reporting verbs in the simple past. (Some are in brackets, others are underlined.)**

Sally Miller:
(state) Climate change is nothing new because it's happening all the time: it always has done, and it always will. So I <u>don't think</u> that the Greens can blame humans for something that's just part of nature.

Mark Farina:
I <u>don't agree</u>. (point out) There's a clear connection between the rise in CO_2 levels that began with the Industrial Revolution and the warming that the world has seen since then. (go on to say) The more CO_2 people throw into the atmosphere, the more temperatures will continue to rise.

Sally Miller stated that climate change was nothing new because it was _____

_____

_____

_____

_____

_____

B Rewrite the questions as indirect questions, using the reporting verbs in brackets. (The reporting verbs should be in the simple past.) Make any other changes that are necessary.

Back in London after the Brussels trip, Julie's friends had lots of questions.

1 **Kate:** 'Does your newspaper often send you on jobs like that?' (ask)

Kate asked if her newspaper often _____

_____

2 **Chris:** 'How long were you away?' (want to know)

_____

3 **Lisa:** 'Did you interview anyone interesting?' (wonder)

_____

4 **Ellie:** 'What did you talk to Matt Radley about?' (inquire)

_____

5 **Tom:** 'Did he answer your questions properly?' (ask)

_____

6 **Jean:** 'Have you written your report yet?' (inquire)

_____

7 **Tom:** 'When can we read it in the paper?' (want to know)

_____

8 **Ben:** 'Where do you think they'll send you next?' (wonder)

_____

C Rewrite the requests, instructions and advice in indirect speech, using the reporting verbs in brackets. Make any other changes that are necessary.

The Brussels trip had been Julie's first big job, so her editor Tony Good wanted a meeting about it. He called Julie and said, 'Come to my office for a chat as soon as you're free.' (tell ... to) 'Could you give me a bit longer so that I can finish my report?' Julie replied. (ask ... to) So Tony gave her a time, and he also said, 'Email me the report before you come to let me have a quick look at it.' (requested ... to) Julie agreed, and then she said, 'Perhaps you could suggest ways I can improve it.' (ask ... to)

The Brussels trip had been Julie's first big job, so her editor Tony Good wanted a meeting about it. He

called Julie and told her to come to his _____

Julie asked _____

So Tony gave her a time, and he also _____

_____

_____

Before the meeting, Tony contacted the Features Editor, Tania Ray, and asked, 'Would you like to come to my office to discuss Julie Branson's report?' (invite ... to) Both the editors liked the report, but Tony said to Julie, 'I think you should reduce it by about 100 words so that we can include a visual.' (advise ... to)

Then he called Alan Carter in the Art Department and said, 'I want you to prepare a visual that will show the fracking process.' (instruct … to) Finally, at the end of the meeting, Julie made a big request. She said, 'Tony, could you send me to find out how local people feel about the fracking project? Please!' (beg … to)

Before the meeting, Tony contacted the Features Editor, Tania Ray, and _____

_____

Both the editors liked the report, but Tony _____

_____

_____

_____

_____

_____

_____

3 LISTENING

→ Rezeption: Hörverstehen, SB S. 225

Julie interviewed local people 1–6 about the fracking project. Listen to their opinions. Then match the opinions a–f to the speakers.

a It's essential to reject the fracking project because of constant noise from heavy vehicles and because of the danger of accidents.

Jenny Wade, student & Greenpeace supporter

Stella King, office worker & expecting 1st child

b Although it will cause temporary local problems, it will bring investments that will produce permanent future benefits.

c It will make a few rich people even richer, but will bring nothing but trouble to the whole community.

Lyn Benson, nursery teacher & mother of two

Brian Fox, 78, retired builder four-time grandfather

d It's wrong to develop new fossil fuel sources. It's essential to rely just on renewable energy sources to protect the future of the Earth.

e It's fine to accept some temporary problems as everything will be quiet and peaceful for many years after that.

Alan Smith, 20, apprentice mechanic

Bob Lowe, jobless engineering worker & father of three

f Renewables cannot produce enough energy yet, so it's very important to generate power till then from a cleaner source than coal or oil.

4 WRITING

→ Produktion: Schreiben, SB S. 228

A The six opinions in 3 are different answers to issues a–c. Match two opposite opinions on each issue.

a Fracking's temporary effects: how important are they? (Opinions _3b_ & ___)

b Who gets what out of the project? (Opinions ___ & ___)

c Fossil fuels – or green renewables? (Opinions ___ & ___)

B Write three paragraphs for Julie Branson's report, one about each issue in 4A. Choose from these reporting verbs, and connect the opposite opinions with *However, …*

> accept ▪ argue ▪ believe ▪ complain ▪ feel ▪ think

Start like this, and continue in your exercise book.

What do local people think about the fracking project? I found that opinions were very varied, and here are just a few of them. Stella King, an office worker who is expecting her first child, thought that it was essential to reject the fracking project because of the constant noise from heavy vehicles and the danger of accidents. However, Bob Lowe, …

A Read the following suggestions for improving air quality and health in a city. Decide which would be:

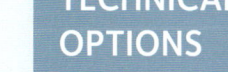
TECHNICAL OPTIONS

* reasonably cheap   * quite expensive   * very expensive ✓

Measures for improving air quality and health			
1 Give out free air pollution monitors for people with respiratory conditions.			
2 Ban cars from the city centre on days with high pollution.			
3 Convert all city buses to hydrogen fuel cell motors.			
4 Produce a free phone app showing air pollution information.			
5 Install pollution monitors at all city traffic lights.			
6 Run an advertising campaign to help car users reduce their pollution.			
7 Remove polluting industries from the city and surrounding area.			
8 Plant more street trees to filter pollution and improve air quality.			
9 Build safe bicycle paths next to all roads.			
10 Install charging stations for electric cars on all city streets.			

B The city council has hired you as a technical consultant. Write two paragraphs. In paragraph 1 support two suggestions, in paragraph 2 reject two suggestions. Follow this structure:

	happy		support	
I am (also)		to say that I		the idea of …ing
	sorry		do not support	

	think		offer	limited		high	
I	believe	it would	produce	useful	benefits at a (very)		cost.
	am sure		create	major		reasonable	

1 WORKING WITH WORDS

A Add vowels (a, e, i, o, u) to form two-word expressions from page 147 of the student's book.

1 grnhs gss _____

2 clmt chng _____

3 nvrnmntl plltn _____

4 glbl wrmng _____

5 ntrl rsrcs _____

6 crbn mssns _____

B Use expressions from A to complete the following text.

When the Industrial Revolution began using _____

_____[1] such as coal and various metals for the mass

production of goods, it was quickly clear that it caused terrible

_____[2], poisoning land, air

and water in the area. However, it now seems that human activities

are also causing much wider damage. Burning fossil fuels is producing

_____[3] in the form of gases,

and these _____[4] are raising worldwide temperatures. This is

_____[5], and it appears to be leading to _____

_____[6], which is likely to have disastrous effects on the world's weather systems.

C Complete the texts with words from the boxes – they are all from pages 147–149 of the student's book.

> ecosystems ▪ forests ▪ exploitation ▪ agriculture ▪ crops ▪ species ▪ farmland

From the earliest systems of _____[1] nearly 10,000 years ago, this vital industry has

grown so much that it now requires the _____[2] of over a third of the planet's land

area as _____[3] in order to feed today's huge human population. Over the years, farmers

have cleared _____[4] and many other natural environments with their ancient wildlife

_____[5] to make room for food _____[6] and animal _____[7] that are

suitable for meat production.

> infrastructure ▪ cooperation ▪ groundwater ▪ diet ▪ consumption ▪ famine ▪ drought ▪ irrigation

Farming requires huge amounts of water, and this requirement keeps growing as the human _____[8]

moves towards greater meat _____[9]. Where there is no easy access to rivers or lakes,

farmers often pump _____[10] to the surface and use that. Again, in dry areas where

_____[11] is a problem, the _____[12] of many people may be needed to build

a large _____[13] of _____[14] channels such as the system that carries

water from northern to southern California. If water supplies fail, the effects can be disastrous, as we have

seen in parts of Africa. Food can no longer be produced, so _____[15] and death soon follow.

2 GETTING IT RIGHT

→ Participles, SB S. 268

Expand and connect the notes. Use the words in column 1 followed by participle clauses.

1	While	(grow up) / London	Joe Dean (love) going / help / aunt & uncle on / farm in / country / school holidays
2	Then before	(go) / college / age / 18	(spend) / summer as / volunteer on / organic farm
3	While	(study) economics for / next three years	(take) summer gardening jobs / make money
4	Before	(get) / 'proper' job at / end of college	(volunteer) / six months at CEFS (Centre for Eco-friendly Farming Studies)
5	Then after	(join) / big financial organization / London	(specialize) / investing in environmentally-friendly agriculture
6	After	(continue) with / work / several years	(start) dreaming / leaving & running / own project
7	Then while	(visit) / aunt & uncle, now in their 60s,	(begin) talking / his ideas & they (invite) him / run / farm for them
8	Since	(take over) / aunt & uncle's farm	(introduce) organic farming & / lot / new techniques

Start like this: *While growing up in London, Joe Dean loved going to help his aunt and uncle on their farm in the country in the school holidays. Then before …*

3 WORKING WITH WORDS

A Add these words from pages 147–157 of the student's book to the mind map.

crops ▪ disease ▪ drought ▪ fertilizer ▪ GM technology ▪ herbicide ▪ hydroponics ▪ livestock ▪ organic practices ▪ pests ▪ pollution ▪ runoff ▪ selective breeding ▪ vertical farms ▪ weeds

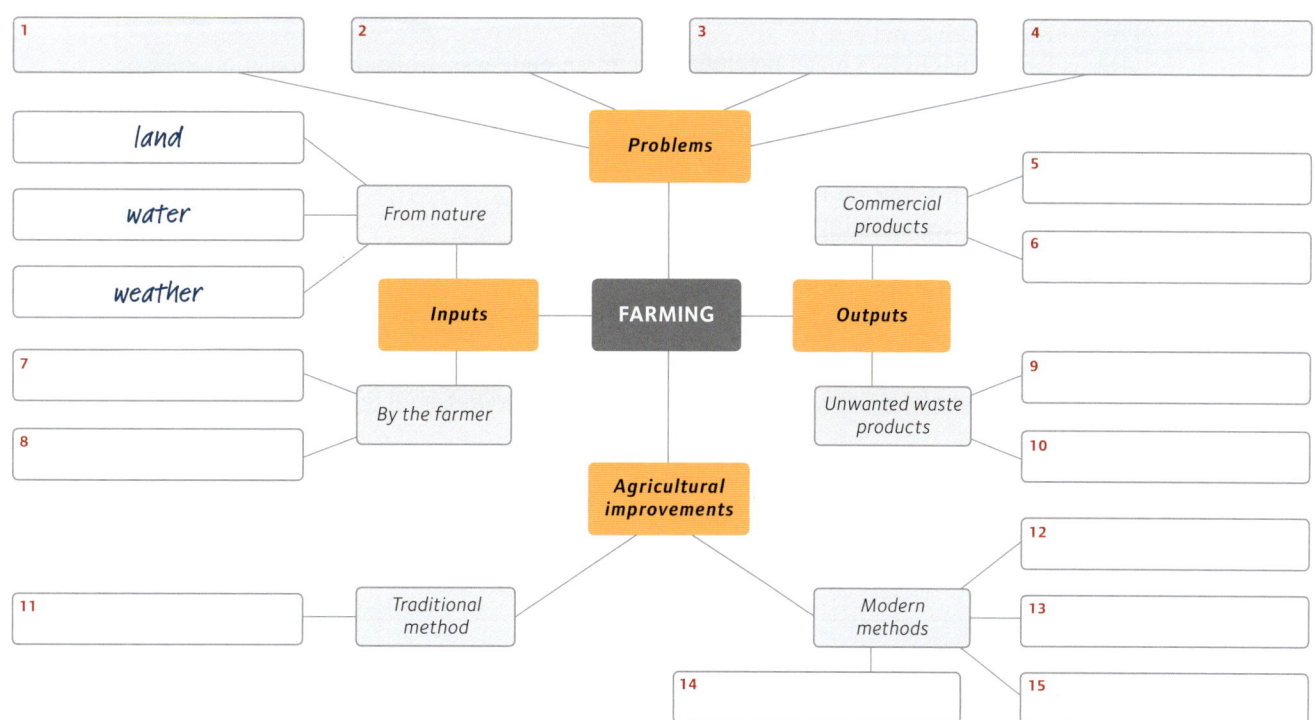

B Now complete these statements with words from the mind map.

1 Inputs to farming from nature include land, water and _____ [1], while inputs by the farmer

include _____ [2] and _____ [3].

2 There is always a danger of damage and destruction, and the farmer faces many _____ [4]

such as _____ [5], _____ [6], _____ [7] and _____ [8].

3 The intended commercial products of farming consist of _____ [9] and _____ [10],

but there are also _____ [11] which include _____ [12]

and _____ [13].

4 Farmers are always trying to make _____ [14]. One traditional

method has always been _____ [15], while modern methods also

include _____ [16], _____ [17],

_____ [18] and _____ [19].

---

4 GETTING IT RIGHT

→ Participles, SB S. 268

Change the relative clauses (starting with *who, which, that*) to *~ing* or *~ed* clauses.

For over 200 years, there have been people who have said that famine would soon kill millions and who have predicted a great reduction in the human population. For example, enormous
5 famines that were predicted in the 1960s for India* and other parts of the world did not happen. Certainly, the scenes of African starvation which have often been shown on our TV screens have been real and terrible enough.
10 However, the fact is that scenarios which warned of hundreds of millions of deaths have not come true – at least, not yet.

This is largely thanks to a green revolution that was created just in time by new varieties of
15 rice, wheat and other crops. These are varieties that were developed by selective breeding in the 1960s and that produce far more food per acre with much greater reliability than before.

However, the productivity push that was
20 given to farming by this revolution is coming to an end, even while the population goes on rising rapidly. The race that is continuing ever more urgently today is to create a new green revolution to get us through the next half century. (190 words) 25

* See e.g. *The Population Bomb*, Paul Ehrlich, published 1968.

For over 200 years, there have been people saying that famine would soon kill millions and _____

_____

_____

_____

_____

_____

5 LISTENING

→ Rezeption: Hörverstehen, SB S. 225

You and your friend are students in London and do not have much money for food. Listen to nutrition expert Dr Sally Carter on the radio as she explains two options.

A Listen to part 1 of the recording and complete the list of prices.

Fast-food prices

2 burgers	£ _____		
2 portions of French fries	£ _____	**Total**	
2 colas	£ _____	**£ _____**	

Supermarket prices

2 portions of chicken	£ _____		
½ kilo of potatoes	£ _____		
Vegetables	£ _____		
Fruit	£ _____	**Total**	
1 litre of milk	£ _____	**£ _____**	

B Listen to part 2 of the recording and complete the answers to the question: 'Why might people prefer to eat fast food?'

a Some people love _____

c Others don't know _____

b Other people don't like _____

d Fast food takes _____

C Listen to part 3 of the recording and complete the notes to answer the question: 'How much time might the two types of meal take?'

Type of meal	Activity		Time (minutes)	
A Fast food	a	Going there & back	15	
	b	_____	_____	Total
	c	_____	_____	_____
B Home-cooked	a	_____		
	b	_____		
	c	_____		Total
	d	_____		_____

Complete the text by inserting the verbs from the box. Change the forms of the verbs where necessary.

check ▪ detect ▪ fly ▪ harvest ▪ have ▪ identify ▪ instruct ▪ look ▪ make ▪ monitor ▪ offer ▪ provide ▪ take (× 2) ▪ weigh ▪ work

TECHNICAL OPTIONS

Taking the guesswork out of farming

Agricultural drones _____[1] a quick, easy and precise way to _____[2] the health of crops. They _____[3] like simple remote-controlled aircraft because they _____[4] just one or two kilos and _____[5] a wingspan of a metre or so. However, two pieces of equipment _____[6] them special: an on-board computer and a high-resolution camera.

The computer _____[7] weather conditions, _____[8] out its own optimal flight path and _____[9] that the drone is functioning properly. The operator just _____[10] it where to go. The camera _____[11] data about plant health. The drone _____[12] over the field at low altitude and _____[13] thousands of images. These images help the farmer to _____[14] problems with weeds, pests etc. They also help him to _____[15] the crops at the best time. Agricultural drones _____[16] the guesswork out of farming.

1 WORKING WITH WORDS

Find words from pages 160 and 161 in the student's book, including the keyword (14).

1 The digital revolution has given us ▬ to information from all over the world.
2 Can I borrow your ▬ to call Ben? I've left mine at home.
3 If you become a ▬ , you'll learn how to write instructions that operate computers.
4 I can't talk now, so could you send me an ▬ with your suggestions?
5 'View' is an important ▬ . It lets you see text in different ways on your screen.
6 I don't use books much: I go ▬ to do most of my research.
7 I haven't got much cash with me, so I'll pay with my ▬ card.
8 If you want to change the print size, ▬ here at the top of the screen.
9 Send Lyn a text ▬ : it's cheaper than phoning.
10 I'm taking my ▬ with me so that I can keep working on the train.
11 At home, we get all our phone, TV and Internet services from just one ▬ .
12 Celtel built up a large ▬ of agents and engineers working across many parts of Africa.
13 The ▬ allows us to share information and communicate with anyone else anywhere.

Keyword: _____

2 WORKING WITH WORDS

A Complete the following. Use these words all starting with *re-*, meaning 'again'.

> rebuild ▪ redevelop ▪ remind ▪ reproduce ▪ rethink ▪ rewrite

1 It was embarrassing when I forgot her name again, and I had to ask her to _____ me.

2 Scientists all over the world are copying our experiments in order to try to _____ our results.

3 The fire damaged the clinic very badly, but they're going to _____ it just as it was before.

4 The digital revolution is changing Africa, and we must _____ our ideas about development.

5 These old 1960s office buildings are terrible. We should pull them all down and _____ the area as a shopping centre.

6 I produced the report before the new information came in. Now I need to _____ it completely.

B Form words that you know with these prefixes meaning 'the opposite of': *in-*, *im-*, *il-* and *ir-*.

_____ dependent _____ legal _____ possible

_____ formal _____ literate _____ regular

C Use opposites from B to complete the following.

1 **A** I suppose it'll be _____ *impossible* _____¹ to contact you in Kenya.

  B Oh no, it's _____² to use the Internet there now.

2 **A** Do farmers have to be _____¹ to be able to use the iCow app?

  B No, it uses voice messages rather than text to help farmers who are _____².

3 **A** Intersat is still an _____¹ company, isn't it?

  B Yes, but it relies on other organizations in various ways. For example, it's _____²
  on TechStar for customer technical support.

4 **A** I hear that out in the villages there were only _____¹ visits by the community
  nurse two or three times a year.

  B Yes, but her visits are much more _____² now – nearly every month.

5 **A** It used to be _____¹ for farmers to sell the animals without any paperwork.

  B Right, but not anymore. That's _____² now, and every animal has to have ID.

6 **A** I hate _____¹ meetings where everyone wears suits. Do I really have to go?

  B Don't worry. They told me that this meeting would be relaxed and very _____².

3 GETTING IT RIGHT

Each sentence contains one mistake. Underline it and then correct it.

4 LISTENING

→ Rezeption: Hörverstehen, SB S. 225

The radio show *The World This Week* is holding a debate about driverless cars, and the audience are being asked to give their views.

18

A Read the list of six jobs in the box below. Then listen and match four of them to speakers 1–4. Add their jobs to column 2.

road construction company director ▪ Accident & Emergency (A&E) hospital nurse ▪ car repair workshop owner ▪ city planning officer ▪ in-car entertainment designer ▪ car insurance salesperson

Speakers	Names & job titles	Opinion	Views on driverless cars
	1 Sylvia Ray _____ _____ _____ _____	☐	**a** Against: reduce demand for / company's services / cause unemployment in / industry
			b For: offer new opportunities / develop communication / other technologies / help drivers use / free time
	2 Ben Miller _____ _____ _____ _____	☐	**c** For: cut / amount of space wasted on city parking / driverless cars / finish one job / go straight to another
	3 Julie North _____ _____ _____ _____	☐	**d** For: greatly reduce / number / road accidents / save precious medical resources / deal / other needs
			e Against: not / possible / repair expensive hi-tech vehicles when / break down / destroy many small businesses like his
	4 Peter Hill _____ _____ _____ _____	☐	**f** Against: if / really so safe / cut / cost / insurance / lots / people working / car insurance business / need to retrain

18

B Read the notes a–f in column 4. Then listen again to the views of speakers 1–4 and match the correct summary notes to the speakers in column 3 'Opinion'.

5 WRITING

→ Produktion: Eine Stellungnahme schreiben, SB S. 234

A Write a comment in two paragraphs. In paragraph 1 agree with one of the speakers from exercise 4. In paragraph 2 disagree with one of the other speakers. Use these ideas:

I (dis)agree with *(name),* the *(job).* I (do not) think … are (an excellent / a terrible) new technology, and I feel (he / she) is (right / wrong) to be (for / against) them. I really (do not) (believe / think it matters a lot) that *(view)* …

_____

_____

_____

_____

_____

_____

_____

_____

_____

_____

B Use the notes in column 4 of exercise 4 to write a paragraph that contrasts a 'for' and an 'against' idea. Structure it like this:

The *(job)* is for driverless cars, but the *(job)* is against them. On the one hand, the *(job)* is (worried / excited) that … On the other hand, the *(job)* is (excited / worried) that …

_____

_____

_____

_____

_____

_____

A Read the text *Galileo: Europe's answer to GPS* on page 170 of the student's book again and then decide whether the following statements are true (T) or false (F), or whether the information is not mentioned in the text (N). Correct the false statements.

TECHNICAL OPTIONS

1	Galileo is not yet fully operational.	☐
2	There will be a total of 30 satellites in the Galileo constellation.	☐
3	There will be one spare satellite in case an operational satellite fails.	☐
4	Ninety per cent of people in the world will be able to access Galileo.	☐
5	Four satellite signals are required to determine a position.	☐
6	Galileo will be more reliable than the US GPS system.	☐
7	Galileo will improve satellite navigation in cities with many tall buildings.	☐
8	Satnav users will have to choose either Galileo or GPS, as they cannot be used together.	☐
9	The ground infrastructure will check that the satellites are sending accurate data.	☐
10	Timing errors of a billionth of a second are considered acceptable.	☐

B Does Europe really need its own satellite navigation system? What is your opinion? Give reasons.

_____

_____

_____

1 WORKING WITH WORDS

Complete the crossword with words from pages 175 and 176 of the student's book. The first letter of
each word has been given to help you.

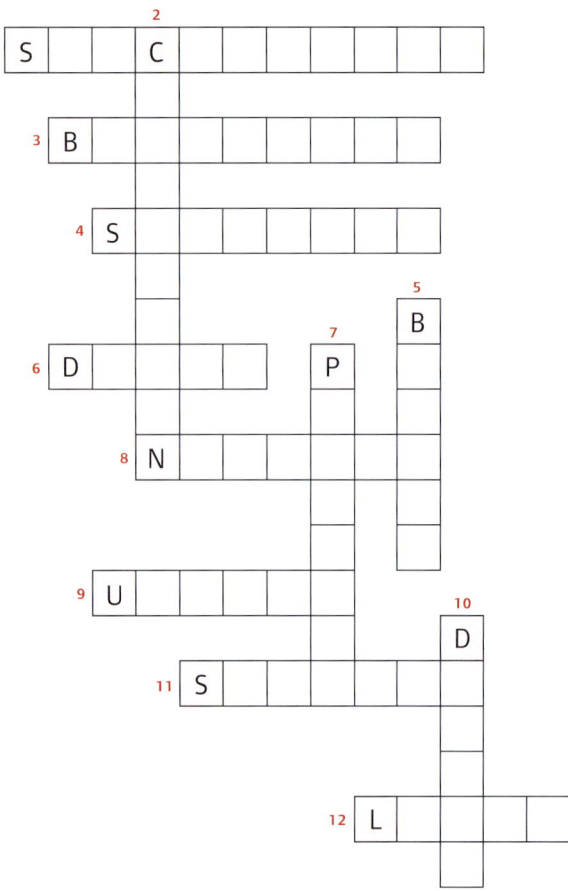

1 If you tick the '■■ data' box, all of your
   computers will have the most up-to-date version
   of these files.
2 To use the cloud, you need an Internet ■■ ,
   of course.
3 ■■ is the amount of data that you can send or
   receive at one time.
4 File ■■ is important: you need to protect your
   data from unauthorized use.
5 'Do I need to keep my own ■■ of vital data?' –
   'It isn't necessary, but it's a good idea.'
6 I thought the files were on my computer's
   hard ■■ , but actually they were in the cloud.
7 An Internet service ■■ is a company that allows
   users to access the Internet.
8 There are 12 computers in my company's ■■ .
   Can they all share the same cloud account?
9 I want to ■■ these large files to the cloud server.
   How long will it take?
10 'Can I use your cloud services on my tablet,
   phone and laptop?' – 'Yes, you can use them
   on any ■■ .'
11 'How much data ■■ does eCloud offer?' –
   'It offers 20GB for free.'
12 ■■ computing is when you keep your data and
   software on your own computer.

2 LOOKING AT THE TEXT

→ Rezeption: Leseverstehen, SB S. 214

Read the text on cloud computing models on page 65 and then read what Amy, Doug, Jon and Lenny
require for their business. Then identify which cloud computing option outlined in the text is best for
them. Give reasons for your choices.

	Best opinion	Reasons
Amy	_____ 1	_____ _____ 5
Doug	_____ _____ 2	_____ _____ 6
Jon	_____ 3	_____ _____ 7
Len	_____ _____ 4	_____ _____ 8

Jon
We're magazine publishers. Several people work on each article – a writer, a researcher, an editor and a designer. We need to make the process more efficient. Also, managing endless software updates and sorting out problems is time-consuming and expensive.

Amy
My company produces training videos for metal working and mechanical engineering. There must be a way to market and sell them without setting up our own store and running a lot of expensive hardware.

Len
Our sales reps are always complaining about not having the latest price lists and product information. Also, if customers have questions that the sales reps can't answer, they have to phone up head office, and that takes time.

Doug
I've written a few successful apps, now I want to make it a full-time career. I want to stay independent, but I don't have time to manage my own web server as well as write software.

CLOUD COMPUTING MODELS
FROM CLOUDSOURCE COMPUTING

Software as a Service (SaaS)

For a small monthly fee, you get access to industry-standard applications and the efficient collaborative environment of the cloud. Work together to create great content. Manage projects effectively with our collaboration tools. Communicate instantly with your sales network via secure messaging. Use our

5   financial management software to centralize and simplify your financial planning, transactions and reporting. We update our applications suite as soon as new versions become

10   available, so you never have to upgrade your software – we do it for you, free of charge.

Platform as a Service (PaaS)

Want to develop your own software

15   and get it to market – fast? Don't want to manage your own web servers? Then look no further than CloudSource Computing. We provide a complete platform for fast software

20   development. Use our runtime environment to run any number of apps, and our database to handle all of the data your apps require. Our identity services manage access for all your developers, testers and end users.

Infrastructure as a Service (IaaS)

Focus on your core competencies without having to worry about setting up and running an expensive

25   data centre. CloudSource Computing provides a complete infrastructure that you can use to run your online business. That includes virtual machines to provide all the computing resources you need, block storage for your data and the networking components to tie everything together. We are responsible for housing, running and maintaining the equipment. So you can concentrate on what you do best – selling great products to your customers.   (252 words)

1 LOOKING AT THE TEXT

→ Mindmaps, SB S. 231

A Read the text *The future of advertising is bright – and DIGITAL* on page 178 of the student's book and then complete the mind map with ideas from the text. Look, for example, at the advantages and disadvantages of different types of signage.

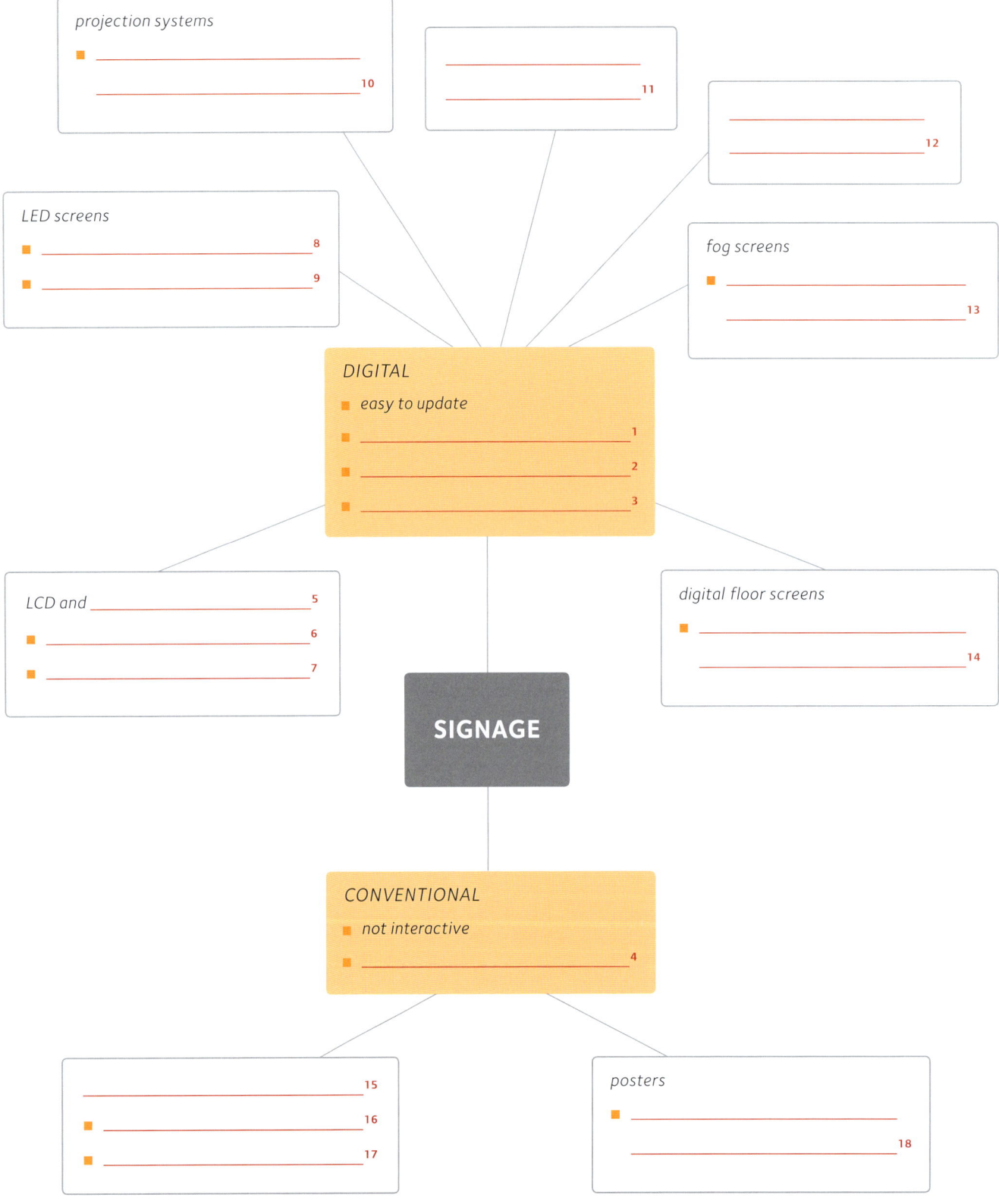

projection systems
- _____
_____ 10

_____
_____ 11

_____
_____ 12

LED screens
- _____ 8
- _____ 9

fog screens
- _____
_____ 13

DIGITAL
- *easy to update*
- _____ 1
- _____ 2
- _____ 3

LCD and _____ 5
- _____ 6
- _____ 7

digital floor screens
- _____
_____ 14

SIGNAGE

CONVENTIONAL
- *not interactive*
- _____ 4

_____ 15
- _____ 16
- _____ 17

posters
- _____
_____ 18

B Now add your own ideas about the technologies mentioned in the text to the mindmap.

2 WRITING A COMMENT

→ Produktion: Eine Stellungnahme schreiben, SB S. 234

The article on page 178 of the student's book was written for an advertising industry magazine and is very positive about digital signage – but is there another side? Write a comment for the magazine's website, giving your opinion about digital signage.

Here are some points to consider:

- All digital signs need electrical power.
- Filling our city streets with moving images could distract car drivers, etc.
- Are there more useful applications for this technology than advertising?

3 LED QUIZ

How much do you remember about LEDs? Do the quiz to find out! Complete the sentences with the correct endings a, b or c. Then go back to the text *How do LED screens work?* on page 180 of the student's book to check your answers.

1 LED stands for …

   a light electric device. ☐
   b light-emitting device. ☐
   c light-emitting diode. ☐

2 Silicon …

   a is the central component of an LED. ☐
   b seals the LED crystal from the air. ☐
   c is attached to either side of the LED crystal. ☐

3 The colour of the light from the LED …

   a depends on the semiconductor material. ☐
   b depends on the current flowing through it. ☐
   c depends on the voltage of the power source. ☐

4 LEDs …

   a produce a lot of light and heat but use little power. ☐
   b produce a lot of light but little heat and use little power. ☐
   c produce little light and heat but use a lot of power. ☐

5 Each LED module …

   a contains three or more LEDs. ☐
   b contains three or fewer LEDs. ☐
   c contains exactly three LEDs. ☐

6 An LED screen contains …

   a blue, yellow and magenta LEDs. ☐
   b red, blue and green LEDs. ☐
   c LEDs of many different colours. ☐

7 Liquid crystals …

   a are a type of LED. ☐
   b do not emit light. ☐
   c are a better light source than LEDs. ☐

1 WORKING WITH WORDS

A Complete the table with the English equivalents of the German expressions. The expressions are all in the text *What is a PASSIVE HOUSE?* on page 181 of the student's book.

1		Klimatisierung
2		Klima
3		Energierechnung
4		Energieeffizienz
5		Umwelt, Umgebung
6		Wärmeverlust
7		Heizung
8		Raumklima, Innenbedingungen
9		Isolation
10		erneuerbare Energiequelle
11		Sonnenenergie
12		Wärmebrücke
13		Lüftung

B Use expressions from part A to complete the FAQs (Frequently Asked Questions) below.

Passive house FAQs

What is a passive house?

It's a building with extremely high _____[1]. The design reduces

_____[2] to a minimum.

Where is the best place to build a passive house?

Anywhere. The passive house design works in every _____[3].

It produces comfortable _____[4] – warm in winter and cool in

summer.

Do I need radiators and other forms of _____[5] in a passive house?

No. The house will stay warm through excellent _____[6] and

through a heat recovery system. Both of these prevent heat from leaving the house.

Do I need _____[7] to keep the house cool in summer?

No. The same systems that keep the house warm in winter keep it cool in summer.

How good is the air quality in a passive house?

Very good. Thanks to a clever _____[8] system, air is exchanged

between the inside and outside without losing heat. →

Do I have to install solar panels or wind turbines for my passive house?

No. _____ [9] like these can be used, but

they are not an essential part of the passive house design.

What are the benefits of living in a passive house?

Many. For example, you will have a comfortable, well-built home and much lower _____

_____ [10] than in a conventional home.

2 PASSIVE HOUSE TECHNOLOGIES

A The diagram below shows a conventional house. Turn the design into a passive house by drawing and labelling passive house technologies on the diagram. Use different colours if possible. Start by drawing and labelling these features on the diagram:

- Three-pane glazing
- Airtight building envelope
- Insulation

B Now add at least three more of the features mentioned in the topic.

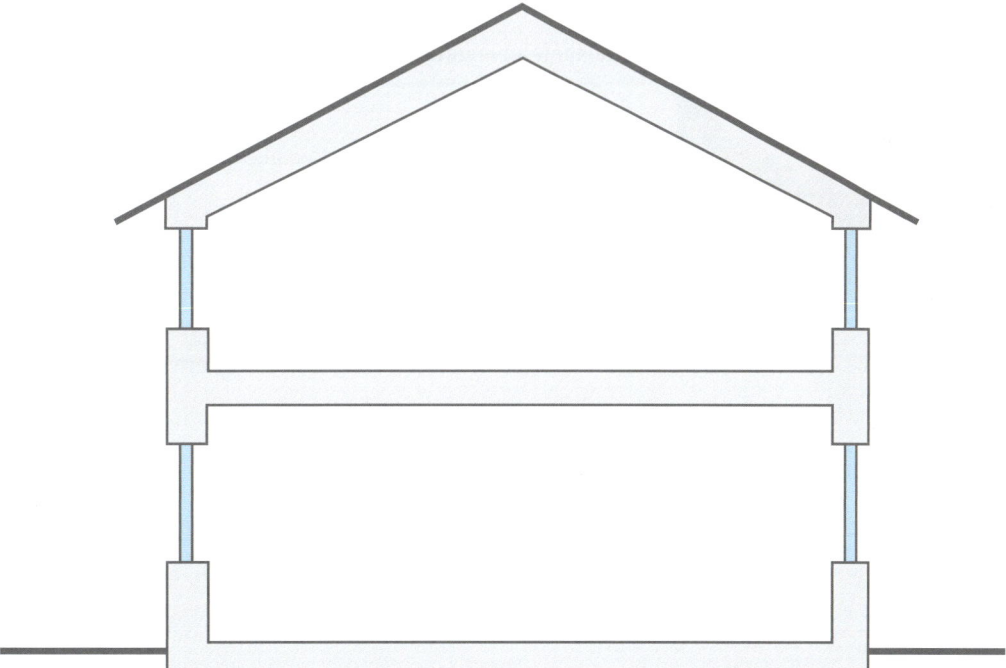

C Write a short explanation to accompany your diagram, explaining how each technology helps to make the building comfortable and energy-efficient.

_____

_____

_____

_____

1 WORKING WITH WORDS

A Complete the table below, using a dictionary if necessary. The words are all from exercise 1 on page 184 of the student's book.

	Noun	Adjective
1		durable
2		ecological
3		laminated
4		long
5	moisture	
6		renewable
7		solid
8	strength	
9		structural
10		sustainable

B Use words from the table in part A to complete the text.

THE NEW TIMBER

Glulam is an engineered timber product, which is made by a _____[1] process. Pieces of timber are glued together to make bigger pieces. It is a way of making timber elements that you can't make in _____[2] timber because of their _____[3] or shape.

5　　Glulam can be used in a whole range of applications – anything from furniture making and kitchen worktops to very large _____[4] elements in buildings and bridges. Wherever steel or concrete beams are used, glulam could be used instead.

10　　When it comes to _____[5], glulam is far better than steel and concrete. Far less energy is required, and unlike steel and concrete, the raw material – trees – is _____[6]. Glulam is also better for forest _____[7] than traditional timber. Smaller trees can be used: it is not necessary to cut down big, old trees to make big glulam beams.

15　　Glulam has 1.5 to 2 times the _____[8]-to-weight ratio of steel. It's also stronger than traditional timber. The _____[9] of glulam depends on the specification: the type of timber, type of glue and type of preservative that are used. With the correct specification it can be used in very tough conditions, e.g. in swimming pool roofs, where it is exposed to high _____[10] levels.　　(205 words)

2 WORKING WITH WORDS

A Find 15 verbs from the topic relating to industrial timber processing in the word square.

T	O	R	O	T	A	T	E	D	E	A	T
S	A	W	N	P	R	E	R	I	N	T	P
C	S	A	D	A	P	R	E	S	S	E	R
T	E	F	A	C	R	A	D	S	T	R	O
E	A	E	R	K	I	M	I	L	L	E	G
S	R	E	E	A	N	I	K	A	S	S	R
T	H	D	F	G	C	L	A	M	P	D	A
E	A	R	F	E	I	E	H	O	A	T	M
P	L	A	N	E	R	D	R	Y	L	I	E
R	I	P	A	N	A	R	A	T	L	L	R
O	N	O	P	E	R	A	T	E	E	T	A
C	U	T	E	T	R	A	N	S	F	E	R

B Use verbs from part A to write captions for these pictures. There may be more than one answer.

1 _____

2 _____

3 _____

4 _____

5 _____

6 _____

7 _____

8 _____

1 WORKING WITH WORDS

Complete the crossword, using the <u>opposites</u> of the words in red. The words you need are all in the text *Speech recognition software* **on page 187 of the student's book. Use a dictionary if necessary.**

1 This system is almost useless because of its inaccuracy.
2 If your pronunciation is very imprecise, the system will have difficulty understanding you.
3 In language, we combine phonemes to form words.
4 The voice recognition in early smartphones was very basic.
5 This appliance requires manual operation.

6 Unlike humans, computers can only process digital data.
7 We don't want the rate of incorrect interpretations to worsen.
8 There are only 40 phonemes in English, but our capacity for inventing new words seems infinite.
9 Speech recognition on this phone require some extra software.
10 The output of the speech recognition software is sent to the software that controls the machine.
11 The speech recognition software makes occasional mistakes.
12 Background noise produces a constant signal.

2 WORKING WITH WORDS

Translate these sentences into English, using idiomatic expressions from the text *Microsoft's "Star Trek"* *voice translator* **on page 189 of the student's book.**

1 Hoffentlich können wir bald die Sprachbarriere beseitigen.

   Hopefully we'll soon be able to _____

2 Das ist eine tolle Idee, aber können wir es wirklich umsetzen?

   That's a great idea, _____

3 Ja sicher: Bald wird Google eine neue Dienstleistung präsentieren.

   Yes, of course: _____

4 Wenn Computer Sprachdienste übernehmen, wird uns der menschliche Kontakt fehlen.

   If robots take over language services, _____

5 Ganz im Gegenteil: Wir werden dadurch bedeutsame Verbindungen schaffen können.

   On the contrary: _____

6 Diese Technologie ist noch ganz am Anfang.

7 Ja, aber sie wird viele Möglichkeiten eröffnen.

3 **LOOKING AT THE TEXT**   → Rezeption: Leseverstehen, SB S. 214

Read the text *Microsoft's "Star Trek" voice translator* on page 189 of the student's book again and then complete the sentences below in your exercise book.

1 In order to understand new life forms, the crew of the Starship Enterprise …
2 Because people speak different languages, they …
3 The new Skype translator is helping to overcome language difficulties by …
4 At the Code conference, Gurdeep Pall was able to show that …
5 Two years previously, the translator had not been able to …
6 Gurdeep Pall believes that the translator has the potential to …
7 For 15 years, Microsoft …
8 Rather than just combining speech recognition, machine translation and speech synthesis in a linear way, Microsoft …

4 **LOOKING AT THE TEXT**   → Rezeption: Leseverstehen, SB S. 214

Read the sentences a–e and then add them to the text *Understanding the brain* in the right spaces. There is one sentence that you do not need.

a To do this they must follow exact instructions (programs).
b Each one is connected to thousands of other neurons.
c However, neural networks are not brains, they are just software models.
d One day, quantum computers may be able to do this better.
e Like neurons they have connections which carry inputs and outputs.
f Then it can do the things that human brains do.

UNDERSTANDING THE BRAIN

A human brain contains about 100 billion neurons. Each neuron is made up of a cell with connections attached to it: several dendrites (carrying inputs to the cell) and one axon (carrying outputs from the cell). [5] Inside a computer, there are transistors – very small switching devices. □[1] That sounds a little like a brain, doesn't it?

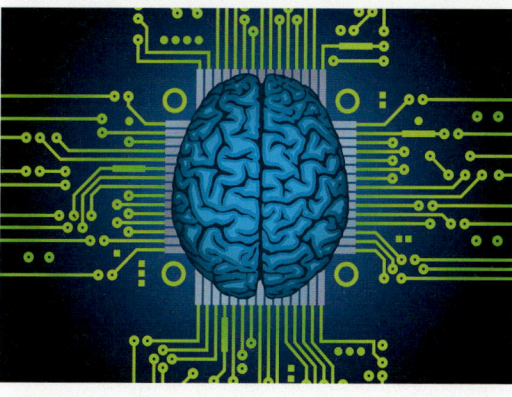

However, computers and brains are completely different in how they process information. The transistors in a computer are wired in simple, serial chains (each one is connected to two or three others to form logic gates). [10] Neurons on the other hand are connected to each other in complex, parallel ways. □[2]

Computers are good at storing very large amounts of data and rearranging it quickly. □[3] Brains, by [15] contrast, learn slowly, but are good at taking independent decisions, learning from mistakes and recognizing patterns.

The idea of a neural network is to make a computer behave like a brain. □[4] Neural networks learn by [20] themselves, in the same way that a brain does. □[5] That is to say, they are made by programming conventional computers to behave like brains. The information inside them means nothing to them.

(188 words)

1 WORKING WITH WORDS

Complete the licence agreement with verbs from the box. These are taken from exercise 1 on page 190 of the student's book. There is one verb that you do not need.

add ▪ agree ▪ alter ▪ copy ▪ create ▪ fix ▪ modify ▪ permit ▪ share ▪ view ▪ work

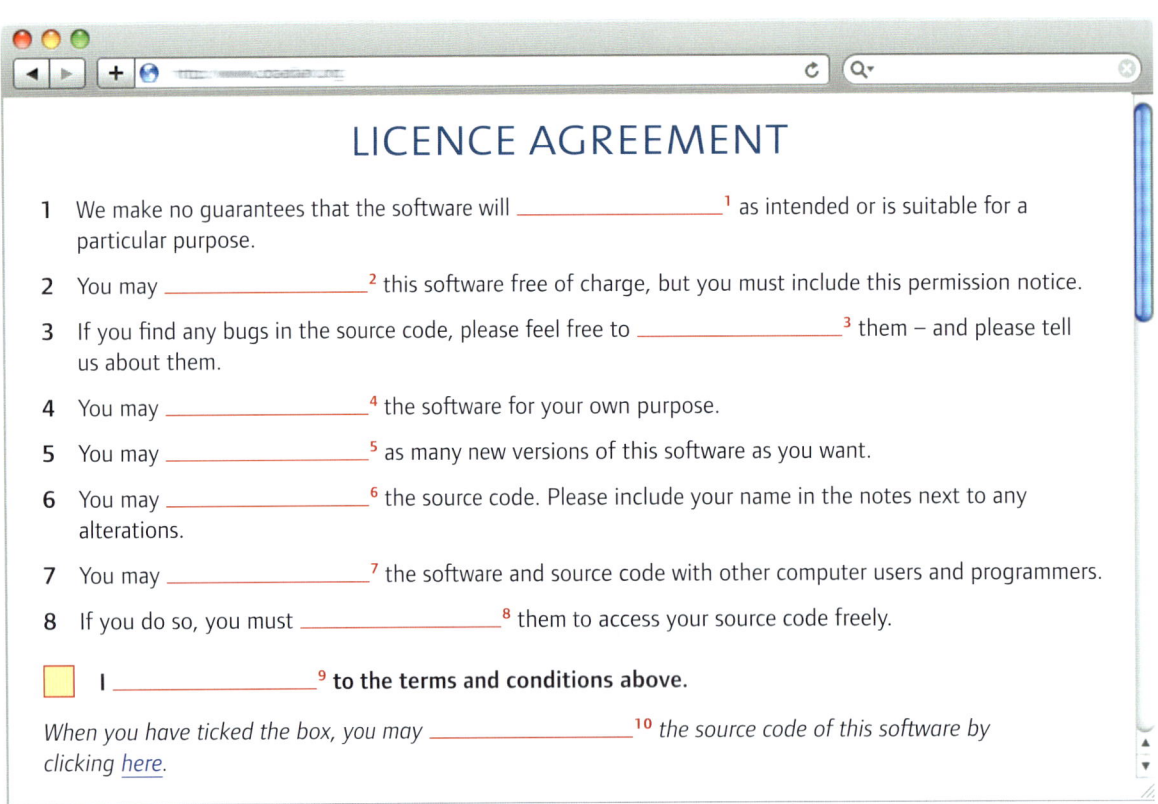

LICENCE AGREEMENT

1   We make no guarantees that the software will _____[1] as intended or is suitable for a particular purpose.

2   You may _____[2] this software free of charge, but you must include this permission notice.

3   If you find any bugs in the source code, please feel free to _____[3] them – and please tell us about them.

4   You may _____[4] the software for your own purpose.

5   You may _____[5] as many new versions of this software as you want.

6   You may _____[6] the source code. Please include your name in the notes next to any alterations.

7   You may _____[7] the software and source code with other computer users and programmers.

8   If you do so, you must _____[8] them to access your source code freely.

☐   I _____[9] to the terms and conditions above.

When you have ticked the box, you may _____[10] the source code of this software by clicking here.

2 MEDIATION

→ Schriftliche Mediation, SB S. 240

Ihre Schule erwägt die Installation neuer, teurer Webdesign-Software auf dem Schulnetz für den Einsatz u. a. im Informatik- und Mediengestaltungsunterricht. Sie wollen die Schuldirektion überzeugen, stattdessen Open-Source Software zu verwenden. Schreiben Sie eine E-Mail auf Deutsch, in der Sie die Argumentation aus dem Artikel *Why open source* zusammenfassen. Übersetzen Sie dabei nicht wörtlich aus dem Text.

WHY OPEN SOURCE?

More control
Having access to the source code gives users and developers more control. You can look at the code to make sure it isn't doing anything you don't want it to do, and you can change parts of it you don't like. That isn't the case with proprietary software.

Fewer bugs and faster updates
Anyone can read and modify the source code of open source software, so it's likely that someone will spot and correct bugs that a program's original authors missed. Because programmers can work on open source software without having to ask anyone's permission, bugs are fixed and upgrades made quickly.

Learn from other programmers
Open source software helps students become better programmers. They can learn to make better software by studying what others have written. They can also share their work with others and get feedback.

More long-term reliability
Many businesses prefer open source software to proprietary software for important, long-term projects. Because the source code for open source software is distributed publicly, users that rely on it for critical tasks can be sure their tools won't disappear or become obsolete just because the original developers stop working on them.   →

5

10

15

20

25

Not just freeware

30 Taking the open source route doesn't mean that you are left without technical support. Many open source software developers charge a fee for software services and support, rather than the software itself. So the software may be free of charge, but you can pay the developer to help you install, use and troubleshoot it.

(215 words)

3 OPEN SOURCE BUSINESS MODELS

Read messages 1–7. Then study the open source software options in the box. Decide which option matches which message.

advertising-supported software ▪ bounties ▪ crowdfunding ▪ delayed open-sourcing ▪ donationware ▪ dual-licensing ▪ optional proprietary extensions ▪ software as a service ▪ support services

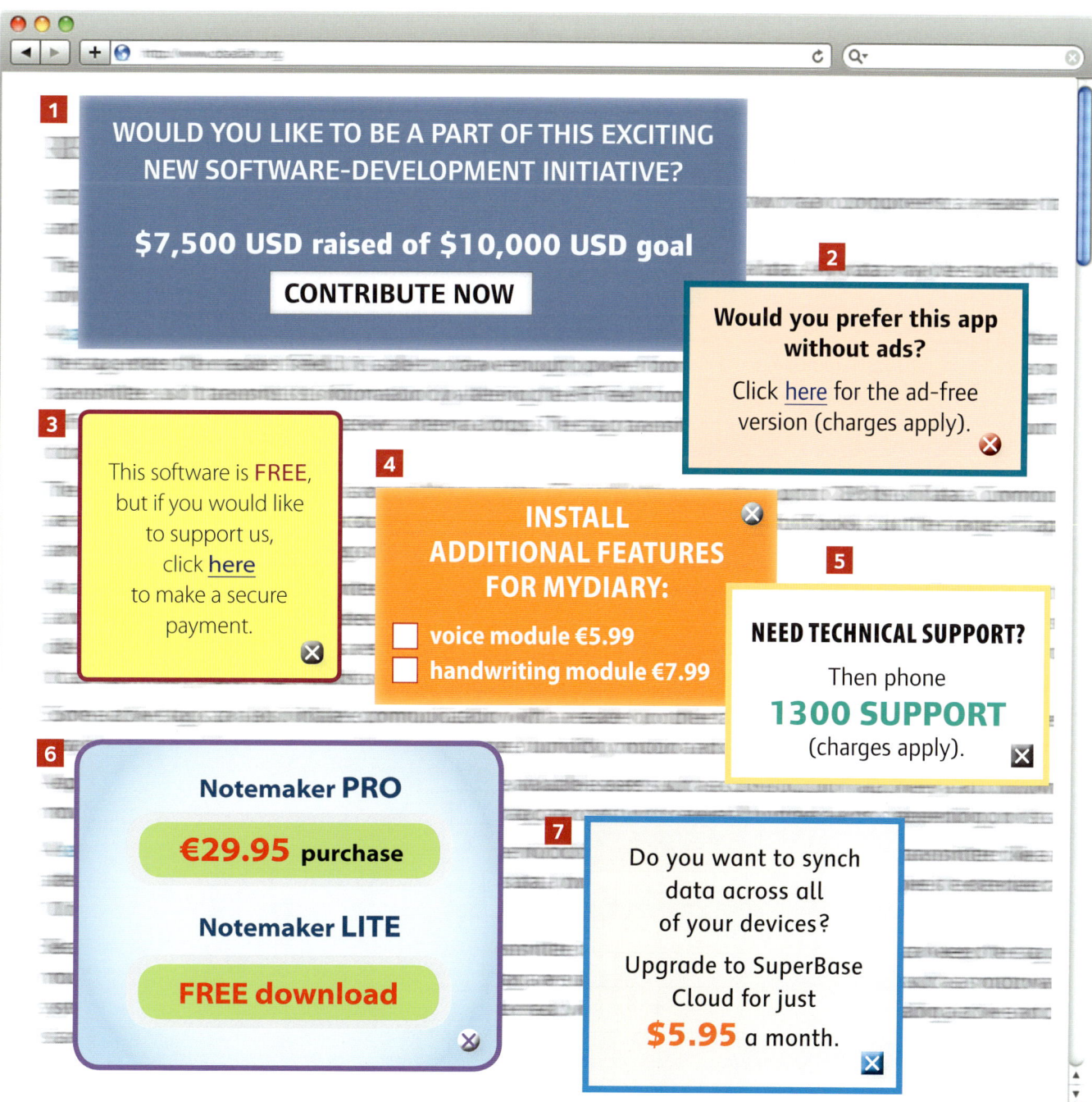

1
WOULD YOU LIKE TO BE A PART OF THIS EXCITING NEW SOFTWARE-DEVELOPMENT INITIATIVE?

$7,500 USD raised of $10,000 USD goal

CONTRIBUTE NOW

2
Would you prefer this app without ads?
Click here for the ad-free version (charges apply).

3
This software is FREE, but if you would like to support us, click here to make a secure payment.

4
INSTALL ADDITIONAL FEATURES FOR MYDIARY:
☐ voice module €5.99
☐ handwriting module €7.99

5
NEED TECHNICAL SUPPORT?
Then phone
1300 SUPPORT
(charges apply).

6
Notemaker PRO
€29.95 purchase
Notemaker LITE
FREE download

7
Do you want to synch data across all of your devices?
Upgrade to SuperBase Cloud for just
$5.95 a month.

1 WORKING WITH WORDS

Complete the puzzle and add the right letters to the shipping label below to find out the details of a planned journey. The words are all from page 193 of the student's book.

1 Consumer goods are usually sent from the factory to a  , and not directly to a shop or store.

```
[ ][ ][ ][ ][ ][ ][ ][ ]
 1        5    18
```

2 Rotterdam is one of the biggest container  in the world.

```
[ ][ ][ ][ ][ ]
 2   10
```

3 If you send the goods tomorrow, when can we expect 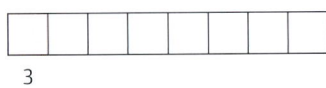 ?

```
[ ][ ][ ][ ][ ][ ][ ]
 3
```

4 Rail transport has greater energy 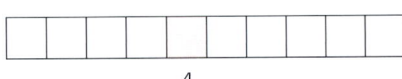 than road transport.

```
[ ][ ][ ][ ][ ][ ][ ][ ][ ][ ]
 4
```

5 London Heathrow is a very busy 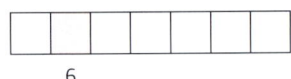 .

```
[ ][ ][ ][ ][ ][ ][ ]
 6
```

6 If  is important, the goods should be sent by air, not sea.

```
[ ][ ][ ][ ][ ][ ]
 7
```

7 A 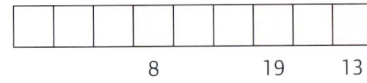 aircraft may transport some goods as well as people.

```
[ ][ ][ ][ ][ ][ ][ ][ ][ ]
    8      19   13
```

8 The less energy we 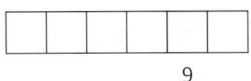 transporting the goods, the better.

```
[ ][ ][ ][ ][ ][ ]
      9
```

9 Increasing costs may make road transport 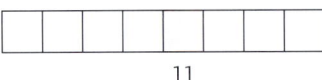 for some goods.

```
[ ][ ][ ][ ][ ][ ][ ][ ]
       11
```

10 The oil company wants to build a  to transport oil from Canada to the US.

```
[ ][ ][ ][ ][ ][ ][ ][ ]
       12
```

11 Computers are an example of high-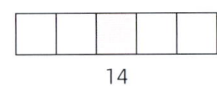 goods.

```
[ ][ ][ ][ ][ ]
    14
```

12 Increasingly, logistics has to consider the 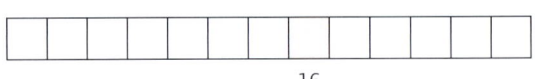 as well as the financial cost of transport.

```
[ ][ ][ ][ ][ ][ ][ ][ ][ ][ ][ ][ ][ ]
             16
```

13 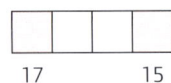 freight is transported in special ships, which can carry large amounts of loose goods.

```
[ ][ ][ ][ ]
 17      15
```

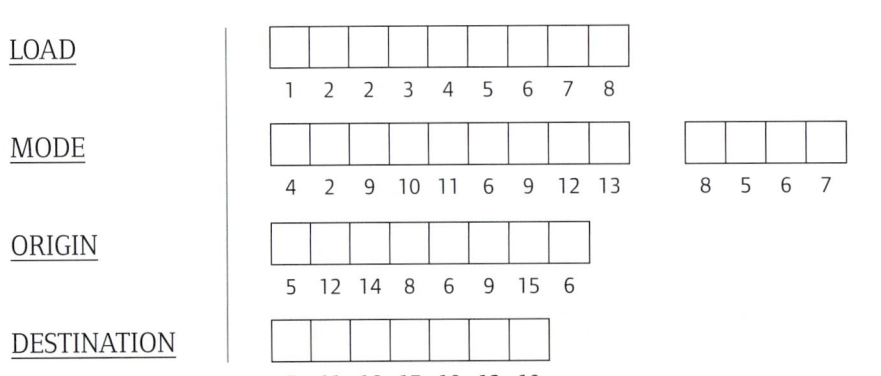

LOAD
```
[ ][ ][ ][ ][ ][ ][ ][ ][ ]
 1  2  2  3  4  5  6  7  8
```

MODE
```
[ ][ ][ ][ ][ ][ ][ ][ ][ ][ ]   [ ][ ][ ][ ]
 4  2  9 10 11  6  9 12 13         8  5  6  7
```

ORIGIN
```
[ ][ ][ ][ ][ ][ ][ ][ ]
 5 12 14  8  6  9 15  6
```

DESTINATION
```
[ ][ ][ ][ ][ ][ ][ ]
 5 11 16 17 18 13 19
```

2 LOOKING AT THE TEXT

→ Rezeption: Leseverstehen, SB S. 214

A Read the text *A shipping revolution in the skies* on page 194 of the student's book and then decide whether the statements 1–6 below are true (T) or false (F), or if the information is not given in the text (N).

1 The first of Mr Pasternak's Aeroscraft airships has already been built. ☐

2 The Aeroscraft will not need an airport runway to land on. ☐

3 The Aeroscraft will travel faster than a ship and carry more cargo than a freight plane. ☐

4 The airship's buoyancy is controlled by compressing air to make it heavier. ☐

5 Mr Pasternak is no longer interested in developing the Aeroscraft for military purposes. ☐

6 He plans to make a smaller version of the Aeroscraft first. ☐

B Read the text *Skysails: bringing wind back to ship propulsion* on page 195 of the student's book and then complete the sentences below with information from the text.

1 The aim of the SkySails system is to _____

2 The SkySails kite is more effective than ordinary sails because _____

3 Although conditions may be variable, the SkySails system can _____

4 Over six years, the SkySails system has been used _____

5 For existing ships, it is possible to retrofit a SkySails system _____

6 The system does not prevent the ship from _____

3 WRITING

→ Einen Aufsatz schreiben, SB S. 234

Write an essay on the subject: 'Rising fuel costs and stricter environmental laws – the end of global freight?' Use ideas from the topic as well as your own ideas and research. Structure your essay like this:

Introduction
A brief statement of the problem and your position

Main part of the essay
- Threats to global freight
- Making freight energy efficient
- New technology

Conclusion
- Summary of the main ideas
- Your opinion

Before you start writing the essay, make notes in English. You may wish to use a mindmap like this to help you to organize your ideas.

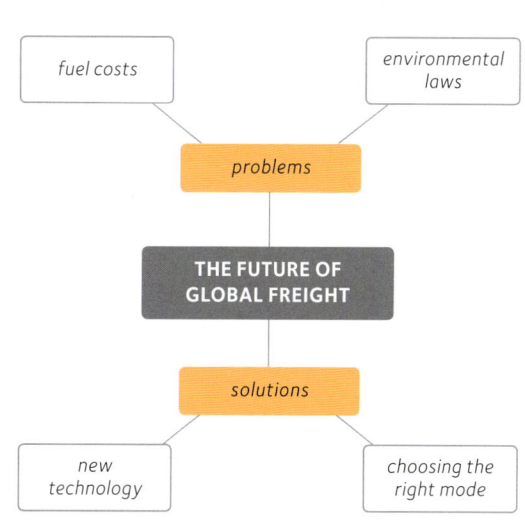

1 WORKING WITH WORDS

A Look at exercise 1 on page 196 and exercise 4 on page 198 of the student's book. Find 19 nouns from these exercises in the word square and write them down in one of the three categories. Then add the German translation for each one.

S	A	M	E	M	O	R	Y	A	D	O	P	B	R
E	T	R	A	N	S	M	I	T	T	E	R	R	E
N	M	E	L	A	N	W	Q	U	A	N	O	A	S
S	U	C	P	W	E	J	O	I	N	T	C	I	I
E	S	E	W	A	E	E	I	K	E	R	E	N	G
R	C	I	A	I	D	T	B	R	S	I	S	Y	H
S	L	V	R	S	I	R	A	A	A	A	F	S	U	T
E	E	E	N	T	E	L	E	C	T	R	O	D	E
L	T	R	O	A	S	A	R	H	R	A	R	T	B
N	I	M	P	L	A	N	T	E	H	M	A	H	R
O	L	D	R	A	C	U	T	S	I	E	R	I	A
S	T	R	E	N	G	T	H	T	E	R	G	G	N
A	R	I	A	S	A	N	E	R	V	E	N	H	A
H	E	A	R	T	H	E	A	R	I	N	G	A	W

1 Five nouns to describe human abilities:

- _____
- _____
- _____
- _____
- _____

2 Eight nouns to describe parts of the body:

- _____
- _____
- _____
- _____
- _____
- _____
- _____
- _____

3 Six nouns to describe cybernetic components:

- _____
- _____
- _____

- _____
- _____
- _____

B **Use words from part A as well as your own ideas to answer these two questions.**

1 Compare and contrast cybernetics and wearable robotics.

_____
_____
_____
_____
_____
_____
_____

2 Describe some potential benefits of cybernetics and wearable robotics.

_____
_____
_____
_____
_____
_____
_____

2 ROBOTIC EXOSKELETON

Annotate the drawing with information from the text _Robotic suit gives shipyard workers super strength_ on page 198 of the student's book.

1 WORD FIELDS

Read the text *Politician's fingerprint "cloned from photos" by hacker* on pages 199–200 of the student's book. Find eleven words and phrases in this text that belong to the following three word fields and write them down in the correct fields.

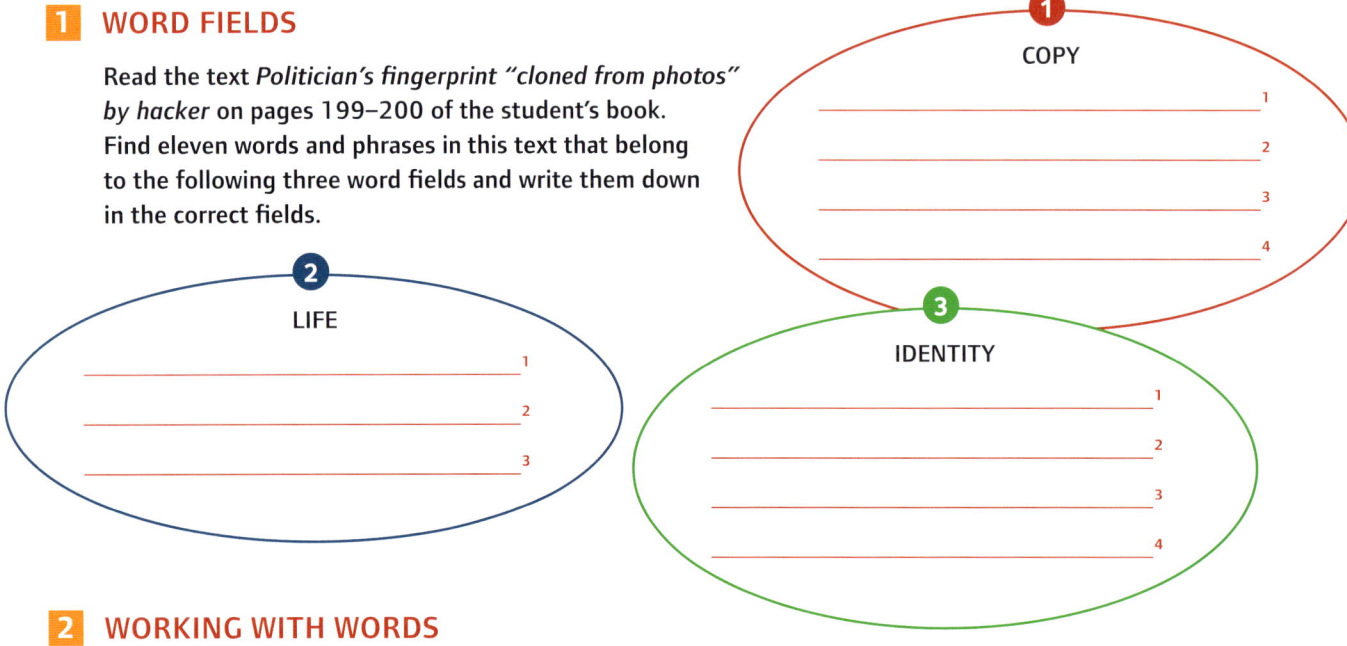

1 COPY
1 _____
2 _____
3 _____
4 _____

2 LIFE
1 _____
2 _____
3 _____

3 IDENTITY
1 _____
2 _____
3 _____
4 _____

2 WORKING WITH WORDS

Complete the text with the English equivalents of the German words in brackets. You can find all of them in exercise 4 on page 200 of the student's book.

Biometrics is the study of measurable biological characteristics. Biometric security systems rely on

_____[1] (*Merkmale*) that can be checked automatically by a computer.

_____[2] (*Fingerabdruck*) recognition systems are the most popular, followed

by face recognition and iris scanning – checking the unique _____[3]

(*Muster*) in the coloured part of a person's eye.

However, static biometric systems like these are no longer considered _____[4]

(*sicher*) enough, as they can all be tricked using an image rather than the real thing. So, systems are

being developed to _____[5] (*messen*) dynamic characteristics, such as the

pitch and rhythm of a person's voice, or their typing speed and _____[6]

(*Rhythmus*) when they _____[7] (*eingeben*) their user ID and password.

As well as comparing a person's _____[8] (*Unterschrift*) to the one on

record, modern systems can analyse the speed and pressure that the writer used.

But technical _____[9] (*Komplexität*) has its problems. Authorized

users may be locked out even when the devices are working properly. This is called a 'false negative'

_____[10] (*Identifizierung*). Furthermore, small changes, maybe even

due to accidents or injuries, can change a biometrics profile.   (172 words)

3 LOOKING AT THE TEXT

→ Rezeption: Leseverstehen, SB S. 214

Read the sentences a–g and then add them to the text about three-factor authentication in the right spaces. There is one sentence that you do not need.

a   This is a biometric, such as finger vein patterns, facial features or iris patterns.
b   The most common passwords are 'password' and '123456'.

c It's easy to work out the password if you know enough about the owner.
d Many users take time to adapt to new technologies.
e The problem is, it's difficult to remember these complicated passwords.
f For this reason, multi-modal security is often used.
g For this reason, banks issue their customers with electronic tokens.

Something you know, something you have, something you are

Some authentication techniques are more secure than others, but it generally is not a good idea to rely on one technique. However secure you think it is, there is the chance that somebody will 'crack' it. ☐ ¹ A common approach is three-factor authentication: something you know, something you have and something you are.

Something you know

5   Passwords are an obvious example of 'something you know'. Unfortunately, people cannot be relied upon to make up secure passwords. ☐ ² That is why better authentication systems prevent you from registering a password which is a common word. You may be required to use a sequence of upper and lower case letters, numbers and special characters like @ and ! ☐ ³ As a consequence, many people write them down.

Something you have

10   To add an extra layer of security, you can add a second factor: something that the user 'has'. ☐ ⁴ These generate a unique access code every time they are used. Sometimes the user must swipe their credit card to gain access to the token, sometimes they must enter their secret PIN via the keypad. Because this layer of security is tied to a physical object, users will quickly notice if it has been stolen.

Something you are

15   These two factors are good enough for most day-to-day security, but if you need really high-level protection, you can add something that the user 'is'. ☐ ⁵ Together, these three factors are very difficult to fake. It is almost always possible to circumvent a security system, but if it requires too much effort, the would-be intruder will look for another, easier victim.

One thing to remember, however, is that ease-of-use is very important and any IT security solution is only as strong
20   as its weakest link – usually the user. ☐ ⁶ So, when banks introduce new security measures, there are usually complaints from customers that they are making life 'too complicated'.   (312 words)

4   WORD FAMILIES

Complete the table below with vocabulary from exercise 6 on page 201 of the student's book. You can use a dictionary for help.

Verb	Adjective	Noun
	1	universality
	2	permanence
3	4	measurability
perform	5	performer/performance
6	acceptable	7
circumvent	circumventable	8
authenticate	9	10
suit	11	12
differ	13	14
	15	accuracy
imitate	imitable	16

1 ANNOTATING A DIAGRAM

Read the words in the three boxes. They are all taken from exercise 1 on page 202 in the student's book. Then label and describe the parts of the electric motor and explain how it works.

Components

coil ▪ copper wire ▪ electromagnet ▪ permanent magnet ▪ rotor ▪ stator

Energy

alternating current ▪ electrical ▪ kinetic ▪ magnetic ▪ polarity ▪ pole

Actions

align ▪ attract ▪ change ▪ repel ▪ rotate

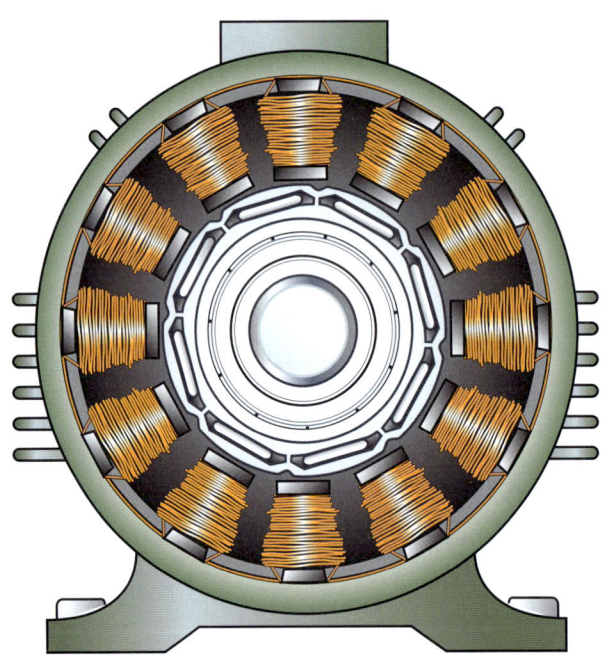

2 WORKING WITH WORDS

Read the text *Hybrid electric vehicles* then explain the highlighted expressions in your own words. The words can be found in exercise 2 on page 203 of the student's book.

HYBRID ELECTRIC VEHICLES

Hybrid electric vehicles [1] have many of the advantages of electric propulsion [2] without its disadvantages. So they are relatively clean and green, but they do not have the same range limitations as pure electric cars. In a nutshell, they have a fuel tank as well as a battery bank.

There are different ways to combine an electric motor and an internal combustion engine [3] in one
5   vehicle. Hybrid electric vehicles can be either mild or full hybrids, and full hybrids can be designed in parallel or series configurations. →

Mild hybrids are also called micro hybrids because they only have a small electric motor. It can't power the vehicle by itself. It allows the petrol or diesel engine to shut off when the vehicle stops at traffic lights or in city traffic, and that improves fuel economy [4]. The electric motor can also be used to assist the engine
10   when rapid acceleration [5] is required. It enables the use of a smaller, more fuel-efficient engine. Full hybrids have more powerful electric motors and larger batteries, which can drive the vehicle on just electric power.

Parallel hybrids connect both the engine and the electric motor to the wheels. The electric motor and the engine can power the vehicle either individually or together. The advantage of that configuration is very good fuel economy, together with good performance [6]. For city driving, the electric motor can be used by
15   itself. For motorway driving, the engine takes over.

Series hybrids use only the electric motor to drive the wheels. The engine is not connected to the drivetrain [7], because it is used only to run a generator, in order to generate electricity for the electric motor. It's a way of giving an electric vehicle an extended range. The engine is small and very fuel efficient. It enables an electric car to go everywhere a petrol-driven car can go without running out of power.   (312 words)

3   COMPARING HEV SYSTEMS

Look at the two diagrams showing two ways of combining an electric motor and a combustion engine in a hybrid electric vehicle. Then describe, compare and contrast these two systems. Use information from the text on hybrid electric vehicles in exercise 2 as well as your own ideas.

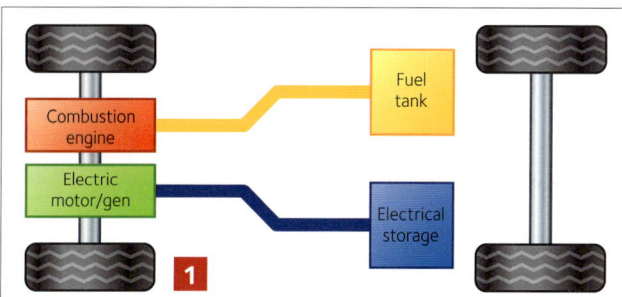

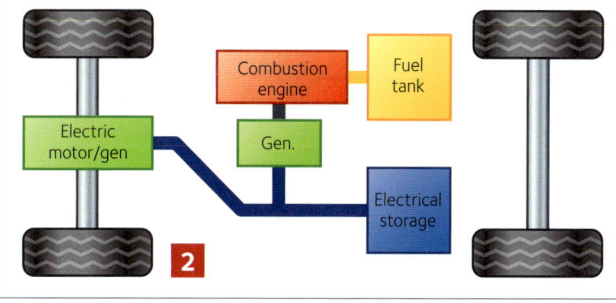

1 WORKING WITH WORDS

A Read the definitions a–o and then match them to the expressions 1–15. All the words are taken from exercise 1 on page 205 of the student's book.

1	application	a	amount of data that can be sent/received at any one time
2	asset	b	communicate something through an electronic signal
3	bandwidth	c	contained within the device
4	conserve	d	distance to which a force can reach
5	detect	e	follow the movements of something
6	field	f	force which can only be felt within a limited space
7	idle	g	how much data a device can contain
8	memory	h	label or device which is attached to something to identify it
9	on-board	i	not doing work
10	power source	j	part of a computer where data is kept
11	range	k	prevent something from being wasted
12	storage capacity	l	object owned by a person or company
13	tag	m	recognize that something is present
14	track	n	something that provides energy
15	transmit	o	use to which something can be put

B Use expressions from part A to complete the sentences below.

1 The _____[1] of the little RFID _____[2] on this box of breakfast cereal is 128 bits.

2 It does not have an _____[1] battery, so it has to draw power from the RFID transponder at the checkout to retrieve data from its _____[2].

3 The _____[1] of a passive RFID transponder is only three metres, so you cannot _____[2] it from a distance.

4 Active transponders are actually _____[1] most of the time, as there is no point in _____[2] data if there isn't a transceiver close enough to receive it.

5 It's important to _____[1] as much power as possible if you only have a small _____[2].

6 That's why this device only becomes active when it _____[1] a signal from an RFID reader – in other words, when it enters the reader's radio frequency _____[2].

2 LOOKING AT THE TEXT

→ Rezeption: Leseverstehen, SB S. 214

Read the article *RFID and the Internet of Things* and write suitable headings for the five sections. The first one has been done for you.

FOCUS ON SUCCESS
5th edition ▪ Ausgabe Technik

FOUNDATION COURSE

Unit 1 The cult of celebrity

1 TALKING ABOUT CELEBRITY

fans, paparazzi, famous, status, star, luxury, legend, stalker, actor, image, autograph, popularity

2 GETTING IT RIGHT

1 A, **2** A, **3** B, **4** A, **5** B, **6** A, **7** A, **8** B

3 GETTING IT RIGHT

1 are	9 am scared
2 love	10 tells
3 have	11 come
4 enter	12 smiles
5 sees	13 relax
6 is not happy	14 says
7 is	15 feels
8 asks	16 win

4 ASKING QUESTIONS

1 What is/What's	4 Why are
2 Where are	5 When do
3 How do	6 Who is

5 BUILDING SKILLS
b

6 LOOKING AT THE TEXT

1 False. Desirée is last month's winner of *Stars for Tomorrow*.
2 False. Patrick is one of the judges on *Stars for Tomorrow*. (He and Desirée are in a relationship.)
3 True
4 False. She accepts that paparazzi take photos when she is not looking perfect / having a bad day.
5 False. The media is full of reports about her personal life.
6 True

7 GETTING IT RIGHT

1 am calling	6 are going too far
2 are you doing	7 Are they trying
3 am reading	8 are only doing
4 is the press making up	9 are walking up
5 are dating	10 am driving into

8 GETTING IT RIGHT

1 am working	5 are looking
2 is going	6 know
3 am having	7 believe
4 stalk	8 love

Unit 2 The world of sport

1 TALKING ABOUT SPORT

A	B
1 participant	1 keep-fit activities
2 spectator	2 do aerobics
3 football	3 go jogging
4 play tennis	4 participant
5 support a team	5 football
6 keep-fit activities	6 spectator
7 do aerobics	
8 go jogging	

2 GETTING IT RIGHT

1 went	4 began
2 played	5 bought
3 won	6 took part

3 GETTING IT RIGHT

A
1 **1** has left; **2** has just moved (signal word: just)
2 **1** has not arrived; **2** has never been (signal words: yet, never)
3 **1** Have you heard; **2** has just joined (signal words: already, just)
4 **1** Have you met; **2** has played (signal word: yet)

B			
1 for		5 since
2 for		6 since
3 since		7 since
4 for		8 for

4 GETTING IT RIGHT

1 charged (earlier today)
2 has not said (up till now)
3 searched (earlier this week)
4 has won (during his career)
5 told (yesterday)
6 drank (before)
7 has sponsored (for)
8 said (this morning)
9 has been (for)
10 gave (before)
11 were (as always)
12 have ever contained (ever)

5 GETTING IT RIGHT

A
1 him
2 me
3 **1** She; **2** them
4 **1** us; **2** it
5 **1** They; **2** We; **3** it

B
9 subject pronouns (sp); 9 object pronouns (op);
6 possessive adjectives (pa)

line 1 my (pa); We (sp)
line 2 Her (op); She (sp)
line 3 It (sp)
line 4 us (op)
line 5 his (pa); Its (pa)
line 6 him (op); me (op); you (sp)
line 7 I (sp); him (op); he (sp); me (op)
line 8 we (sp); his (pa); us (op); them (op)
line 9 their (pa); They (sp)
line 10 you (sp); me (op); your (pa)

6 BUILDING SKILLS

A/B
Expressions we hear: 1, 3, 4, 5, 6, 8, 9
Expressions we don't hear: 2, 7

C

Jane:
1 does aerobics
2 home
3 heart, lungs
4 stress
5 (too) expensive

Will:
1 goes swimming
2 at local swimming pool
3 work-out
4 sleep well
5 weight
6 slim and stay slim

Lily:
1 plays volleyball
2 at college
3 lose
4 burns up
5 friends
6 get to know people
7 good friends

Unit 3 Fashion and brand power

1 TALKING ABOUT BRANDS

A
1 slogan
2 fashionable
3 price
4 product
5 affordable
6 quality
7 advertising
8 values
9 choice
10 famous

B
brand names

2 GETTING IT RIGHT

A
1 carefully
2 simply
3 beautiful
4 usually
5 similar
6 expensive; cheaply

B
1 Lucy <u>frequently</u> shops at the outlet store.
2 Jim <u>always</u> dresses well.
3 My new computer <u>suddenly</u> stopped working.
4 The coffee in that café is <u>usually</u> good.
5 I <u>really</u> want these boots.

3 USING A DICTIONARY

1 choose
2 choosy
3 cost
4 costly
5 affordability
6 afford

4 GETTING IT RIGHT

A/B
1 bigger than
2 biggest
3 lighter than
4 as heavy as
5 heavier than
6 as long as
7 longest
8 cheapest
9 more expensive than
10 most expensive
11 best
12 most difficult

C
The NeatPhone because it's the lightest and it looks the nicest.

5 COLLOCATIONS

1 low
2 victim
3 new
4 copies
5 house

6 BUILDING SKILLS

A
(Lösungsvorschläge)

Giving an opinion	(Personally,) I think / feel / believe (that) … It seems to me (that) … If you ask me, … My (own) view of the matter / problem is …
Giving reasons	You see, … The reason is (simply) (that) … The main / basic reason is (that) … The thing is, you see, …
Agreeing with an opinion	Yes, I agree. (Absolutely.) That's (quite) right / true. I couldn't agree more. Yes, that's just how I see it. That's exactly my own view / opinion …
Disagreeing with an opinion	I don't agree. (Well,) as a matter of fact, … Actually, / In fact, I think (that) … (I'm afraid) I can't accept that.
Interrupting	I'm sorry to interrupt / break in, but … Excuse me for interrupting / breaking in, but … Can I (just) stop / interrupt you there for a moment?

B

1	view	3	reason	5	afraid
2	opinion	4	disagree	6	interrupt / believe

C–E
(freie Lösungen)

Unit 4 Leisure and free time

1 TALKING ABOUT FREE TIME ACTIVITIES
(freie Lösung)

2 GETTING IT RIGHT

A

1	Will you come	5	Will I see
2	will probably be	6	won't have
3	won't be	7	will help
4	will cancel	8	will be able to

B

1 I am going to train for the next marathon.
2 Mark and Mindy are going to go backpacking in Australia next summer.
3 Some pupils are going to start a film club next term.
4 The snooker championships are going to be held in Paris this year.
5 Are you really going to buy a motorbike?
6 I'm not going to go shopping for the rest of the year.

3 BUILDING SKILLS

A

1	is lying	4	are watching	7	is standing
2	is	5	hungrily	8	angry
3	looks	6	are flying	9	is shouting

B
b

4 LOOKING AT THE TEXT

1 F, 2 F, 3 F, 4 T, 5 F, 6 T

5 BUILDING SKILLS
(Lösungsvorschlag)

Hallo …

Tut mir leid, dass du wieder Stress mit deiner Mutter hast! Ich habe kürzlich in einem Blog gelesen, dass uns allen ständig gesagt wird: „Als ich in deinem Alter war …!" Wie wahr! Die Leute, die das sagen, wissen echt, wie sie einem den Tag ruinieren …

Was diese Leute nicht verstehen, ist, dass heute eben nicht gestern ist! Wir machen ja immer noch total viel mit unseren Freunden, aber wir machen es eben anders – im Netz. Naja, ok, das ist dann nicht so direkt von Angesicht zu Angesicht, aber wir kommunizieren ja genauso viel, machen gemeinsam Hausaufgaben, tauschen Ideen aus usw. Und dabei lernen wir die ganze Zeit auch immer wieder neue Leute kennen!

Warum können ältere Leute nicht mal akzeptieren, dass sich die Welt weiter dreht und verändert? Und vielleicht sollten sie ab und zu mal darüber nachdenken, dass sie auch mal jung waren …

6 GETTING IT RIGHT

1	any	6	many	11	many
2	much	7	any	12	many
3	little	8	many	13	a few
4	a few	9	a little	14	much
5	some	10	some		

7 BUILDING SKILLS
(Lösungsvorschlag)

The photo shows a girl dressed in summer clothes, sitting on a platform next to a railway track. The tracks are in the countryside and are leading to a forest. The girl is alone, and she has a backpack and a sleeping mat with her. She is looking at a map. The activity shown is backpacking in a natural environment. The girl in the photo may have chosen this activity because she likes to be alone and free.

I would enjoy doing this activity. I love being free in the outdoors, wandering through the countryside, discovering new places. When I'm on my own, I can give all my attention to the place I'm visiting.

I would not enjoy doing this activity. Going backpacking alone in the countryside would bore me. I prefer to do things with my friends. And when we go on holiday, we want fun and action.

MAIN COURSE

Unit 5 The virtual world

1 WORKING WITH WORDS

1	Regardless	5	engage	9	exceeds
2	adult	6	isolated	10	avoid
3	several	7	poll		
4	appear	8	average		

2 LOOKING AT THE TEXT

1 The average British person spends one hour on social media per day.
2 Women check their pages more often than men.
3 More than 3.6 million Britons use Twitter for more than two hours a day.
4 Facebook was voted the most popular social media site by 59% of people polled.
5 People avoid being isolated by spending several hours online every day.
6 Rebecca Dye is the social media manager at *first direct* online bank.
7 Rebecca Dye means that people don't write letters or emails and don't phone each other or meet up in person as much these days.
8 Rebecca Dye's company will interact more with its customers on social media.

3 BUILDING SKILLS

A

c

B

1 isolation, frustration, loneliness, felt need to use Facebook app
2 focus on the household (housework), spend more time with family (daughter)

4 GETTING IT RIGHT

1	went	11	looked
2	opened	12	Were
3	checked	13	did
4	found	14	didn't
5	was	15	couldn't
6	thought	16	rang
7	was	17	was
8	found	18	left
9	didn't	19	understood
10	sat	20	had to

5 LISTENING

A

1 False. Margaret Green phones Catherine Seale.
2 True
3 False. She thinks they're in London.
4 False. She's in her car.
5 False. She told him not to have any parties.
6 True
7 False. A boy is trying to break in.
8 False. Gatecrashers are blocking the street.
9 True
10 False. The riot police stopped the people wrecking the front garden.

B

1	vomiting	4	gatecrashers
2	skylight	5	revellers
3	trash	6	flight

C

(Lösungsvorschlag)

Margaret Green drove her son Jamie to the party at Christopher Seale's house. When she arrived, she saw hundreds of young people in the street and in the front garden. The music coming out of the house was extremely loud. Jamie got out of the car, walked up to the house, rang the doorbell and waited. Nobody opened the door, so he pushed it open and went inside.

When the door opened, Mrs Green saw young people dancing wildly and shouting. Suddenly, she heard a crash. It came from the roof. She looked up and saw a teenager standing on the roof. The next thing Mrs Green saw was the riot police. They jumped out of their vans and started to break up the crown outside the house. Mrs Green then realised that things were out of control, so she phoned Catherine Seale. She thought the Seales were out for the evening. She didn't know that they were on holiday in France.

6 GETTING IT RIGHT

1 hasn't used
2 used
3 **1** has changed; **2** made
4 **1** weren't; **2** felt
5 **1** told; **2** were
6 spent
7 hasn't been
8 has changed
9 **1** has started; **2** has done
10 **1** told; **2** played

TECHNICAL OPTIONS

A

1	i	4	j	6	f	8	e	11	a
3	g	5	b	7	d	10	h	12	c

(Lösungsvorschlag)

2 to change information that is in code into ordinary language so that it can be understood by anyone
9 kept hidden from others / something that is known about by only a few people and not told to others

B

(Lösungsvorschlag)

Bob uses asymmetric encryption to send Alice a message. Alice has a public and a private key, which are created using the same algorithm. Alice's public key is not encrypted and is available to everybody, so Alice can share it with Bob and he uses it to encrypt his message to Alice. When Alice receives the message, she uses her unique private key to decrypt it. This key is secure and can only be used by her.

Unit 6 Advertising

1 LOOKING AT THE TEXT

A

1	e	3	i	5	a	7	d	9	h
2	g	4	c	6	j	8	f	10	b

B

1 False. Few people recycle their glass.
2 False. It gives you points.
3 True
4 False. It is much more successful.
5 True
6 False. It's on the ground.
7 True
8 False. In one day people threw in 72kg of rubbish.

2 BUILDING SKILLS

Correct order: d, f, i, h, b, j, c, l, k, g, e, a

3 LISTENING

A/B

A Definition	B Description
Product	top brand perfume and cosmetics
Promotion	special reductions of up to 40%
Price	£40 for 50 ml of top brand perfume; £12 for a 75 ml top brand deodorant stick
Place	in-flight only

4 GETTING IT RIGHT

A

1 I'm sure wearables will be a great success in the near future.
2 We are launching the whole range in Edinburgh on Monday.
3 Each member of my team is going to demonstrate a different sort of wearable.
4 I'm going to wear a waterproof Android watch.
5 We're having a press conference at 9 am.
6 We believe that demand for wearables will double in the next six months.

B

1 we're/I'm going to introduce
2 they'll make
3 We're/I'm going to start
4 you'll be
5 you'll see
6 is competing
7 She's taking
8 she'll win
9 we're/I'm going to ask
10 will win

5 BUILDING SKILLS

A

1 7 May 1946
2 10 (13 incl. MiniDisc, MP3 player and Android Walkman)
3 PlayStation network was hacked (77 million accounts compromised)

B

1 Famous inventions
2 World market
3 Mobile entertainment
4 Major setbacks

C

(Stichworte)

1 brought out transistor radio, changed name to Sony
2 to access the world's largest consumer market
3 light and portable transistor radio and Walkman enabled people to listen to radio and music anywhere, not just in one place
4 laptops and PCs

6 BUILDING SKILLS

1	gives	5	shows
2	has increased	6	has risen
3	rose	7	is
4	went	8	haven't stopped

TECHNICAL OPTIONS

1 T, 2 F, 3 N, 4 F, 5 T, 6 F, 7 T, 8 T, 9 T

2 Beacons will send messages to customers' phones when they enter the store or walk past it.
4 Customers can chose to accept or ignore the messages.
6 Customers will see messages customized to their preferences and location in the store.

Unit 7 Family and beyond

1 WORKING WITH WORDS

A

1	borrow	5	noisy
2	long-distance	6	forget
3	extended	7	together
4	criticize	8	huge

B

1 1 local; 2 long-distance
2 1 noisy; 2 quiet
3 1 remember; 2 forgot
4 1 together; 2 separately
5 1 extended; 2 nuclear
6 1 huge; 2 tiny
7 1 borrow; 2 lend
8 1 criticize; 2 praise

2 GETTING IT RIGHT

A

1 who came to England first
2 which was very poor
3 which paid very little
4 which would offer a better future
5 who was hiring workers for a UK textile company
6 who were offered jobs
7 which followed their arrival
8 who never gave up on anything

B

1 which made us decide to
2 she knew she might soon lose
3 which was doing badly
4 the company had already got rid of
5 who had to go next
6 the EU financial crisis hit very badly
7 who pushed for us to move here
8 I've been most worried about

3 WRITING AN INFORMAL LETTER

53 West Road
Dublin 22
Ireland

29th May, 20…

Dear Grandma and Grandpa

This is to say a big 'thank you' for the money you kindly sent me for my birthday. I'm going to put it towards some beautiful shoes I really, really want! I'll be able to show you them when we get home for Christmas next month. I can't wait for that because I miss you all and the family so much. So do Mum, Dad and Sam.

Well, I must stop now and run to catch the post. Thank you again!

Lots of love
Lisa

4 WORKING WITH WORDS

A

1	in	2	in/at	3	in	4	at

B

1	at	6	in front of	11	above
2	near	7	behind	12	across
3	opposite	8	beyond	13	below
4	next to	9	around	14	In/On
5	Between	10	on		

5 GETTING IT RIGHT

1	were living	9	was looking for
2	weren't getting on / didn't get on	10	were
3	was cleaning up / cleaned up	11	was trying
		12	opened
4	had	13	had to
5	kept	14	was looking forward
6	were all cooking	15	looked
7	had	16	was
8	started	17	shouted / were shouting
		18	agreed

6 BUILDING SKILLS

1	Keighley	5	7 Bow Road, Wendcot
2	Carole Elisabeth	6	AL7 8NB
3	17	7	07765188399
4	13th October		

TECHNICAL OPTIONS

A

Words from snake: acquire, answer, clean, clean, do, feed, fetch, load, operate, perform, pick, water

1	clean	7	answer
2	water	8	pick
3	feed	9	clean
4	fetch	10	do
5	operate	11	acquire
6	load		

B

(Lösungsvorschlag)

Today we had friends over for dinner so the robot was very busy. He started the day by cleaning the whole house, including the floors and toilet, so that the house was perfect for our guests. He fed the dog for us so that we could concentrate on cooking a good meal. Then he tidied the kitchen up when we were finished. In the evening, he opened the door when our friends arrived, and then when we had eaten, he loaded the dishwasher for us.

Unit 8 Entering the world of work

1 LISTENING

1	16
2	–
3	community service group
4	art, English, sport: basketball and football
5	chemistry, biology
6	baby-sitting
7	work placement in a kindergarten, an old people's home or a hospital
8	17
9	top DJ, DJ headliner at the Ultra Music Festival in Miami
10	DJ incl. *Your Mum's House* night club
11	sport, (body-building)
12	all other subjects, especially history
13	Saturday job in a jeans shop; worked in a tattoo studio
14	learn a musical instrument or study music, stay on at school and take exams

2 LOOKING AT THE TEXT

A

1	one month minimum
2	€1,000 + tips + overtime
3	cottage in hotel complex
4	free
5	(keine Angabe)
6	max. €300 for return airfare from home country

B

1	application	5	waiter/waitress
2	leisure	6	willing
3	experience	7	located
4	tip	8	range

3 BUILDING SKILLS

(freie Lösung)

4 WORKING WITH WORDS

1	gradual	5	property
2	workforce	6	requires
3	challenge	7	filing cabinet
4	downsize	8	Human Resources

5 GETTING IT RIGHT

A

1 won't have
2 don't apply
3 send
4 'll/will tell
5 contact

6 'll/will put
7 change
8 'll/will be
9 won't find
10 wait

B

1 'd/would be
2 had
3 worked
4 'd/would deal
5 'd/would be

6 saw
7 'd/would accept
8 meant
9 Would you take
10 came

6 BUILDING SKILLS

A

1 There are several questions to think about when discussing
2 In my opinion
3 firstly
4 secondly

5 Another point to consider is this:
6 On the one hand
7 on the other hand
8 As a consequence
9 On the whole
10 To conclude

B

(freie Lösung)

TECHNICAL OPTIONS

1 b   2 f   3 e   4 d   5 a

Unit 9 Multiculturalism

1 BUILDING SKILLS

C

(Lösungsvorschläge)

1 He grew up in an Afro-Caribbean community / among Jamaicans / in an area he calls 'the Jamaican capital of Europe'.
2 He could not read or write when he left school at the age of 13.
3 The BBC poll showed that he was one of the country's most-loved poets / He was voted the UK's third most-loved poet.
4 This might surprise us because he attacks many things that are part of British culture.
5 He refused the (offer of the) OBE because he is against anything that has a connection with the British Empire.

2 WORKING WITH WORDS

A

1 performance
2 poetry, poem

3 politics
4 song

B

1 singer
2 songs
3 politicians

4 politics
5 performer
6 performances

7 poet
8 poems

3 GETTING IT RIGHT

1 If unemployment had not been so high in Britain, Tom would have found work without much difficulty.
2 If he had got a job in the UK, he would have stayed in Britain quite happily.
3 If things had gone well for him, he would not have wondered about work in other countries.
4 If he had never been to Australia, he is certain he would never have thought about working somewhere so far away.
5 If he had not looked for work there though, he would have missed the perfect job for him – as a tour guide for visitors.
6 If he had not taken a tour group up the Gold Coast, he would never have met the perfect girl for him, and champion surfer Jenny would never have become the love of his life!

4 GETTING IT RIGHT

1 had gone
2 gave
3 had expected
4 had never visited
5 began
6 was
7 had experienced
8 received

9 had happened
10 learned
11 had disappeared
12 read
13 had been
14 explained
15 had finally found

5 LISTENING

1 14.1   2 31.1   3 5   4 8   5 13

6 BUILDING SKILLS

A

1 rose
2 under
3 almost exactly
4 reached
5 little change
6 increase

7 rapidly
8 around
9 approximately
10 downwards
11 fall
12 less than

B

1 fall
2 upwards
3 rose / increased

4 rapidly
5 over / more than
6 approximately / almost exactly

C

(Lösungsvorschlag)

Since 2012, the figures have risen again to levels that the country last saw over a century ago. The latest statistics show that the immigrant population has continued to rise and has reached (00.0) million, approximately (00)% of the present US population of (00.0) million.

TECHNICAL OPTIONS

A

1 A world leader in high-speed rail
2 *Lösungsvorschlag:* Other technological advances
3 The secret of China's success

4 How it all began
5 A familiar pattern
6 *Lösungsvorschlag:* A different approach
7 Risks, but rich rewards

B
1 high-speed (lines 2, 3, 12, 15)
2 advanced (line 5)
3 manufacturing (line 5)
4 renewable (line 6)
5 heavy machinery (line 6)
6 achievements (line 8)
7 contract (lines 12, 22)
8 compete (line 21)

Unit 10 Helping others

1 WORKING WITH WORDS

1	producer	**7**	accountancy
2	charity	**8**	to empower
3	to donate	**9**	amazing
4	donor	**10**	safe
5	complaint	**11**	companionship
6	sponsorship	**12**	homeless

2 BUILDING SKILLS

A
1	the Netherlands (or the UK)	**3**	Turkey and France
2	the USA	**4**	the UK
		5	Germany

B
1	percentage	**3**	place	**5**	column	**7**	twice
2	clearly	**4**	ranks	**6**	value	**8**	half

C
(Lösungsvorschlag)

Whereas private American individuals donate the most money to help others, their government donates the least money. The UK government is the biggest giver donating 0.72% of GNI and UK individuals are the second biggest givers with individual giving at 0.73% of GDP. While French individuals donate the least money, the French government gives twice as much as the US government with 0.41% of GNI compared to 0.19%. The Turkish government gives almost twice as much (0.42%) than private individuals in Turkey (0.23%) whereas the Australian government actually gives almost half as much (0.34%) as Australian individuals do (0.69%).

3 LOOKING AT THE TEXTS

A
1 True
2 False. They were 200 km away (from the British Embassy).
3 Not in the text
4 False. They were strong because they were taught to think of the needs of others first.
5 Not in the text
6 False. They were inspired by Gandhi, who always wore flip-flops.

7 False. It's a registered charity.
8 True

B
1	siblings	**4**	strength	**7**	survival
2	advice	**5**	humanitarian	**8**	charity
3	hitchhiked	**6**	orphanages		

4 LISTENING

1	b	**3**	c	**5**	b	**7**	a
2	a	**4**	a	**6**	b	**8**	c

5 GETTING IT RIGHT

A
1	I've [have] asked	**9**	She hasn't fallen
2	Have I asked?	**10**	We've [have] felt
3	I haven't asked	**11**	Have we felt?
4	You've [have] driven	**12**	We haven't felt
5	Have you driven?	**13**	They've [have] worn
6	You haven't driven	**14**	Have they worn?
7	She's [has] fallen	**15**	They haven't worn
8	Has she fallen?		

B
1 I've [have] been asking
2 Have I been asking?
3 I haven't been asking
4 You've [have] been driving
5 Have you been driving?
6 You haven't been driving
7 She's [has] been falling
8 Has she been falling?
9 She hasn't been falling
10 We've [have] been feeling
11 Have we been feeling?
12 We haven't been feeling
13 They've [have] been wearing
14 Have they been wearing?
15 They haven't been wearing

C
1	have written	**6**	has donated
2	have sold	**7**	has started
3	have been selling	**8**	has been working
4	has been wearing	**9**	's/has been serving
5	has bought	**10**	have bought

TECHNICAL OPTIONS

1	fuel	**6**	basic
2	gravity	**7**	pulley
3	upgrade	**8**	supply
4	frame	**9**	catalyst
5	lightweight	**10**	modify

Unit 11 Global reach

1 WORKING WITH WORDS

A
1	an order	**3**	contact	**5**	action
2	a contract	**4**	quality		

B

1	made a mistake	**6**	filled the position
2	fills a need	**7**	make a complaint
3	take place	**8**	take advice
4	lost heart	**9**	lose sight of
5	raise a question	**10**	raise our prices

2 GETTING IT RIGHT

A

1 Coffee is grown organically by farmers from all over the Gumutindo district.
2 Then the coffee is brought to the new central production facility.
3 There, quality and quantity are checked by highly-trained senior staff.
4 Then the raw coffee is processed in carefully-controlled conditions.
5 After that, the coffee is packed by the Cooperative's new, automated equipment.
6 Finally, the finished product is sent to Mombasa for export to Europe and America.

B

The ACE FURNITURE factory here in Virginia has been closed by the company owners in New York, and 200 workers have been thrown out of their jobs. The decision was made last summer, but the workforce was not told till last month. All the equipment from the Virginia plant will be sent to a new factory in Indonesia, and the same furniture will be produced there for a quarter of the pay.

But when production is moved offshore like this, American jobs are exported, too, and the American economy is damaged. If every US factory is closed, the US economy will be completely destroyed. Then who will all those 'made in Asia' products be bought by?

3 BUILDING SKILLS
(Lösungsvorschlag)

The cartoon shows a manager and one of his workers in the manager's office. He is sitting at his desk, and he is telling his employee that he is going to fire him. He is explaining that the employee has been replaced by someone in China who is better at his job and who is also cheaper to employ.

This is an ironic comment on globalization's effects on ordinary working people's lives in the West. It reminds us that the developed economies are no longer competitive with economies in the Far East, and that many US and European jobs have been exported to the developing world. Because of this, Western workers are faced with an uncertain future in the world of work.

The manager is sitting comfortably, and he is talking to the other man apparently without any sympathy. The cartoonist is attacking the way that business destroys people's lives without any human feeling. As far as the manager is concerned, the employee is just a piece of equipment that he is replacing with a better piece of equipment.

4 LISTENING

A

		B	
1	500 (no change)	**8**	remained unchanged
2	500 – 0	**9**	rapid fall
3	0 – 1,000	**10**	climbed rapidly
4	1,000 – 1,500	**11**	steady increase
5	1,500 – 1,600	**12**	slight further increase
6	1,600 – 1,400	**13**	declined steadily
7	1,400 – 800	**14**	sharp further decrease

5 BUILDING SKILLS

A

(freie Lösung)

B

In the first half of Year 3, sales increased slowly from zero to 500 kilos (per month). Then in the second half there was a steady further rise to 1,500 kilos (per month). In the first half of Year 4, sales climbed only slightly to a (monthly) total of 1,700 kilos. But since then there has been a rapid growth in sales from 1,700 to 3,000 kilos (per month).

TECHNICAL OPTIONS

A

1 polyethylene outer tube
2 Mylar® tape
3 steel wires
4 aluminium foil
5 polycarbonate inner tube
6 copper tube
7 silicone gel
8 optical fibres

B

a	5	**c**	7	**e**	2	**g**	6
b	3	**d**	4	**f**	1	**h**	8

Unit 12 Changing society

1 WORKING WITH WORDS

A

daytime TV, entry-level job, job application, middle management, minimum wage, pay packet, production assistant, retail industry, university degree, welfare system

B

1	minimum wage	**6**	entry-level job
2	retail industry	**7**	university degree
3	production assistant	**8**	job applications
4	middle management	**9**	daytime TV
5	welfare system	**10**	pay packet

2 GETTING IT RIGHT

A

1	needn't	**4**	don't have to	**7**	can't	**10**	might
2	should	**5**	must	**8**	have to		
3	can	**6**	shouldn't	**9**	may		

B

1 **1** haven't been able to; **2** can
2 **1** could; **2** couldn't
3 **1** can't; **2** was able to
4 **1** couldn't; **2** was able to

3 LISTENING

A

Name: Peter North, age: 83, years at WPRH: 2
Wife: Lucy (died 12 years ago)
Children: 3 – 2 sons & 1 daughter
Grandchildren: 6 – ages from 18 to 2
Interests: art class, music (mostly jazz), day trips

B

1 T, **2** F, **3** F, **4** F, **5** T, **6** F, **7** T

C

2 He lived on his own for ten years, before moving to Windsor Park two years ago.
3 He moved to Windsor Park because it was getting hard to look after everything.
4 His two sons and his daughter all have families.
6 They took him out to a restaurant.

4 GETTING IT RIGHT

Rules for visitors

1 Whenever possible, visits should be planned for normal visiting hours. (However, visits may be allowed at other times by special arrangement.)
2 Please note that sometimes a visit may not be allowed if a resident is very unwell.
3 Visitors must be signed in at reception.
4 We are sorry, but pets cannot be brought into the building.
5 You are welcome to eat with us, and visitors' meals can be ordered by phone or email 24 hours in advance.
6 All communication with staff is very welcome, but nurses should not be interrupted when preparing residents' medications.

5 BUILDING SKILLS

a	2	**c**	1	**e**	3
b	6	**d**	5	**f**	4

TECHNICAL OPTIONS

Lösungsvorschläge

1 Electronic pointing devices, sip-and-puff systems, speech recognition programs: Electronic pointing devices will help David to use a computer by using ultrasound, infrared beams or tracking devices.
A sip-and-puff system allows him to use a computer by breathing in and out, while a speech recognition program would enable him to give computer commands by speaking.
2 Braille displays, screen readers, speech recognition programs: A Braille display would allow Chloe to read the content of the screen by forming Braille characters. A screen reader describes to her what is on the screen, while a speech recognition program allows her to give computer commands by simply speaking.
3 Customized keyboards, joysticks and trackballs, light signals, on-screen keyboards: A customized keyboard can be adapted for use with arthritic hands. Joysticks and trackballs allow Margie to move the cursor on screen by using her feet or chin. Light signals allow her to see that an email has arrived or a command has been carried out.
An on-screen keyboard would enable her to select keys by using different devices other than her hands.
4 Customized keyboards, touch screens, on-screen keyboards: A customized keyboard can be adapted for Callum so he can use it despite his problems with fine motor skills. A touch screen allows him to use a computer by directly touching the screen, so he does not require fine motor skills either.
An on-screen keyboard would enable him to select keys by using different devices other than his hands.

EXAM PREPARATION

Unit 13 The challenges of the modern state

1 LOOKING AT THE TEXT

A

b

B

(Lösungsvorschläge)

1 Young girls are leaving the UK to become jihadi brides in the Middle East. They run away from home and seldom come back.
2 They have launched a campaign called 'Making A Stand' to stop young girls from running away. (The campaign includes a letter describing the conditions the girls will live under in an ISIS caliphate.)
3 According to the ISIS leader, a young Western woman can expect a new life and a chance to contribute to the creation of a pure Islamic state. Women can expect a variety of jobs and responsibilities, such as joining the all-female moral police force to make sure women keep to the specific ISIS interpretation of Sharia law.
According to *Making A Stand*, a young woman can expect to be married from the age of 9 and to be kept veiled and out of sight. She can expect to be treated as a second-class citizen, and to lose her individuality and dignity. She will be unable to either fulfil her dreams in the caliphate or return to the West.
4 A young woman might have been born in the UK and have enough money, but still feel socially isolated. She might suffer from depression and feel like she doesn't belong in the West because of restrictions on how Muslims can practise their religion. A young woman might decide to run away and become a jihadi bride because of personal and political reasons, but also because of naive romanticism.

2 WRITING

(freie Lösung)

3 WORKING WITH WORDS

A			B		
	1	terrorist		1	fulfil
	2	remind		2	terrorists
	3	succeed		3	freedom
	4	fulfil		4	restrictions
	5	freedom		5	practise
	6	treat		6	dignity
	7	dignity		7	reminds
	8	promise		8	succeed
	9	migrant		9	treat
	10	violence		10	violence
	11	restriction			
	12	practise			

4 LISTENING

1 b   2 c   3 b   4 c   5 a   6 a

5 GETTING IT RIGHT

1	to open	7	using
2	to download	8	changing
3	to shop	9	to be
4	giving	10	to have / having
5	doing	11	to lose
6	to provide	12	having

6 BUILDING SKILLS

1 If you ask me
2 The main reason is
3 What's your view on
4 I couldn't agree more
5 Well, as a matter of fact
6 I'm afraid I can't accept
7 I see what you mean (or: There's some truth in what you say)
8 there's some truth in what you say (or: I see what you mean)
9 Let me put it in another way
10 do you see what I mean
11 So is the basic idea that
12 I'm sorry to interrupt, but

TECHNICAL OPTIONS

1	particles	5	transformers
2	magnetic field	6	damage
3	electrical grid	7	vulnerable
4	currents	8	monitor

Unit 14 Energy and the environment

1 WORKING WITH WORDS

1	lift	4	stop	7	opportunity
2	hugely	5	appear		
3	reason for	6	grew		

2 GETTING IT RIGHT

A

(Lösungsvorschlag)

Sally Miller stated that climate change was nothing new because it was happening all the time: it always had (done), and it always would. So she didn't think that the Greens could blame humans for something that was just part of nature.

Mark Farina did not agree. He pointed out that there was a clear connection between the rise in CO_2 levels that had begun with the Industrial Revolution and the warming that the world had seen since then. He went on to say that the more CO_2 people threw into the atmosphere, the more temperatures would continue to rise.

B

1 Kate asked if/whether her newspaper often sent her on jobs like that.
2 Chris wanted to know how long she had been away.
3 Lisa wondered if/whether she had interviewed anyone interesting.
4 Ellie inquired what she had talked to Matt Radley about.
5 Tom asked if/whether he had answered her questions properly.
6 Jean inquired if/whether she had written her report yet.
7 Tom wanted to know when they could read it in the paper.
8 Ben wondered where she thought they would send her next.

C

The Brussels trip had been Julie's first big job, so her editor Tony Good wanted a meeting about it. He called Julie and told her to come to his office for a chat as soon as she was free. Julie asked him to give her a bit longer so that she could finish her report. So Tony gave her a time, and he also requested her to email him the report before she came to let him have a quick look at it. Julie agreed, and then she asked him to (perhaps) suggest ways she could improve it.

Before the meeting, Tony contacted the Features Editor, Tania Ray, and invited her to come to his office to discuss Julie Branson's report. Both the editors liked the report, but Tony advised Julie to reduce it by about 100 words so that they could include a visual. Then he called Alan Carter in the Art Department and instructed him to prepare a visual that would show the fracking process. Finally, at the end of the meeting, Julie made a big request. She begged Tony to send her to find out how local people felt about the fracking project.

3 LISTENING

1	d	3	b	5	c
2	a	4	f	6	e

4 WRITING

A

a 3b & 6e;   b 2a & 5c;   c 1d & 4f

B

(Lösungsvorschlag)

What do local people think about the fracking project? I found that opinions were very varied, and here are just a few of them.

Stella King, an office worker who is expecting her first child, thought that it was essential to reject the fracking project because of the constant noise from heavy vehicles and the danger of accidents. However, Bob Lowe, a jobless engineering worker and father of three, felt that it was fine to accept some temporary problems as everything would be quiet and peaceful for many years after that.

Lyn Benson, a nursery teacher and mother of two, believed that although it would cause temporary problems, it would bring investments that would produce permanent future benefits. However, Alan Smith, aged 20 and an apprentice mechanic, complained that the project would make a few rich people even richer, but that it would bring nothing but trouble to the whole community.

Jenny Wade, a student and a Greenpeace supporter, argued that it was wrong to develop new fossil fuel sources, but that it was essential to rely just on renewable energy sources to protect the future of the Earth. However, Brian Fox, aged 78, a retired builder and four-time grandfather, accepted that renewables could not produce enough power yet, so it was very important to have power till then from a cleaner source than coal or oil.

TECHNICAL OPTIONS

A

(freie Lösung)

B

(möglicher Anfang)

I am happy to say that I support the idea of banning cars from the city centre on days with high pollution. I believe it would offer useful benefits – and at a very reasonable cost. I am also happy to support …

Unit 15 Feeding the world

1 WORKING WITH WORDS

A
1 greenhouse gases
2 climate change
3 environmental pollution
4 global warming
5 natural resources
6 carbon emissions

B
1 natural resources
2 environmental pollution
3 carbon emissions
4 greenhouse gases
5 global warming
6 climate change

C
1 agriculture
2 exploitation
3 farmland
4 forests
5 ecosystems
6 crops
7 species
8 diet
9 consumption
10 groundwater
11 drought
12 cooperation
13 infrastructure
14 irrigation
15 famine

2 GETTING IT RIGHT

While growing up in London, Joe Dean loved going to help his aunt and uncle on their farm in the country in the school holidays. Then before going to college at the age of 18, he spent the summer as a volunteer on an organic farm. While studying economics for the next three years, he took summer gardening jobs to make money. Before getting a 'proper' job at the end of college, he volunteered for six months at CEFS. Then after joining a big financial organization in London, he specialized in investing in environmentally-friendly agriculture. After continuing with this work for several years, he started dreaming of leaving and running his own project. Then while visiting his aunt and uncle, now in their sixties, he began talking about his ideas, and they invited him to run their farm for them. Since taking over his aunt and uncle's farm, he has introduced organic farming and a lot of new techniques.

3 WORKING WITH WORDS

A
1–4 disease, drought, pests, weeds
5 + 6 crops, livestock
7 + 8 fertilizer, herbicide
9 + 10 pollution, runoff
11 selective breeding
12–15 GM technology, hydroponics, organic practices, vertical farms

B
1 weather
2 fertilizer
3 herbicide
4 problems
5–8 disease, drought, pests, weeds
9 +10 crops, livestock
11 unwanted waste products
12 + 13 pollution, runoff
14 agricultural improvements
15 selective breeding
16–19 GM technology, hydroponics, organic practices, vertical farming

4 GETTING IT RIGHT

For over 200 years, there have been people saying that famine would soon kill millions and predicting a great reduction in the human population. For example, enormous famines predicted in the 1960s for India and other parts of the world did not happen. Certainly, the scenes of African starvation often shown on our TV screens have been real and terrible enough. However, the fact is that scenarios warning of hundreds of millions of deaths have not come true – at least, not yet.

This is largely thanks to a green revolution created just in time by new varieties of rice, wheat and other crops. These varieties developed by selective breeding in the 1960s produce far more food per acre with much greater reliability than before.

However, the productivity push given to farming by this revolution is coming to an end, even while the population goes on rising rapidly. The race continuing ever more urgently today is to create a new green revolution to get us through the next half century.

5 LISTENING

A
2 burgers: £4.80
2 portions of French fries: £3.20
2 colas: £1.80
Fast-food price total: £9.80

2 portions of chicken: £3.10
½ kilo of potatoes: £0.60
Vegetables: £3.80
Fruit: £1.20
1 litre of milk: £0.90
Supermarket price total: £9.60

B
a   Some people love this sort of food.
b   Other people don't like cooking.
c   Others don't know how to cook.
d   Fast food takes less time and trouble.

C
A   *Fast food*
a   Going there & back: 15
b   Ordering: 5
c   Eating: 15
Total: 35

B   *Home-cooked*
a   Shopping: 45
b   Preparing: 45
c   Eating: 20
d   Washing up & tidying up: 15
Total: 125

TECHNICAL OPTIONS

1	offer	9	checks
2	monitor	10	instructs
3	look	11	provides
4	weigh	12	flies
5	have	13	takes
6	make	14	identify
7	detects	15	harvest
8	works	16	take

Unit 16 Technology

1 WORKING WITH WORDS

1	access	8	click
2	mobile	9	message
3	programmer	10	laptop
4	email	11	provider
5	function	12	network
6	online	13	Internet
7	credit	14	communication

2 WORKING WITH WORDS

A
1	remind	3	rebuild	5	redevelop
2	reproduce	4	rethink	6	rewrite

B
independent, illegal, impossible, informal, illiterate, irregular

C
1   **1** impossible; **2** possible
2   **1** literate; **2** illiterate
3   **1** independent; **2** dependent
4   **1** irregular; **2** regular
5   **1** legal; **2** illegal
6   **1** formal; **2** informal

3 GETTING IT RIGHT

1   is waiting / I'll (I will) lend
2   had to go / he was able to
3   has Carl been doing / He's been
4   a few / two pairs of trousers
5   was signed / must be paid
6   had already gone / I was waiting
7   told me / now she is/she is now
8   Did you go / I'm going to spend/I'm spending

4 LISTENING

A/B
1   (A&E) hospital nurse; opinion d
2   road construction company director; opinion a
3   car insurance salesperson; opinion f
4   city planning officer; opinion c

5 WRITING

A
(Lösungsvorschlag)

I agree with Sylvia Ray, the A&E hospital nurse. I think driverless cars are an excellent new technology, and she is right to be for them. I really believe that they will greatly reduce the number of road accidents and save precious medical resources, which can then be used to deal with other needs.

I disagree with Ben Miller, the road construction company director. I do not think driverless cars are a terrible new technology, and I feel he is wrong to be against them. I really do not think it matters a lot that they will reduce demand for his company's services and cause unemployment in his industry.

B
(Lösungsvorschlag)

The in-car entertainment designer is for driverless cars, but the car repair workshop owner is against them. On the one hand, the designer is excited that they will offer new opportunities to develop communication and other technologies that will help drivers use their free time. On the other hand, the workshop owner is worried that it will not be possible to repair expensive hi-tech vehicles when they break down, and that this will destroy many small businesses like his.

TECHNICAL OPTIONS

A

1 T, 2 T, 3 F, 4 N, 5 T, 6 N, 7 T, 8 F, 9 T, 10 N

3 There will be three spare satellites (one in each plane).
8 Satnav users will be able to use Galileo and GPS together as they will be interoperable.

B
(freie Lösung)

Topic 1 Cloud computing

1 WORKING WITH WORDS

1	synchronize	7	provider
2	connection	8	network
3	Bandwidth	9	upload
4	security	10	device
5	backup	11	storage
6	drive	12	Local

2 LOOKING AT THE TEXT

1 IaaS
2 PaaS
3 SaaS
4 SaaS
5 Amy needs a complete infrastructure for handling large files as well as an online store. She says she doesn't want to run expensive hardware and the text says you don't have to worry about that with IaaS.
6 Doug wants to develop software but not run web servers. PaaS provides a complete platform for software development and says you don't need to manage your own web server.
7 Jon needs collaborative tools because a lot of people work on the articles and the text says that SaaS has an efficient collaborative environment. He also doesn't want to update software, so SaaS is good as it automatically upgrades your software free of charge.
8 Len needs better communications with his sales reps and SaaS offers instant communication via secure messaging. He also says that the sales reps don't always have the latest price lists. SaaS offers software to centralize documents (financial planning, transactions and reporting) so that should help Len.

Topic 2 Digital signage

1 LOOKING AT THE TEXT

A

1–3	interactive, moving images, sound
4	difficult to update
5	plasma screens
6 + 7	high definition, great picture quality
8 + 9	good visibility, low energy use
10	use buildings as screens at night
11 + 12	holographic displays, water screens
13	move images like objects
14	floors/pavements
15	neon signs
16 + 17	expensive, easy to break
18	fall apart because of wind, rain and sun

B
(freie Lösung)

2 WRITING A COMMENT

(Lösungsvorschlag)

I read your article about digital advertising and was interested to see how positive the article was. However, I think there are other points of view to consider here. In my opinion, there are also negative aspects to digital signage. Firstly, all digital signs need electric power. That means a huge amount of electricity is used to light up all these digital signs. As a result, these signs must be damaging the environment. Another point to consider is safety. In my view, there are too many moving images on our streets and these can distract drivers and cause a lot of accidents, injuries and deaths. Furthermore, is there nothing more useful that we can do with this technology? One example might be cutting down long-distance business travel by using holographic displays and fog screens for virtual meetings across the globe. To sum up, I think that digital signage is not always a good thing and should be thought about more carefully.

3 LED QUIZ

1	c	3	a	5	a	7	b
2	a	4	b	6	b		

Topic 3 Passive houses

1 WORKING WITH WORDS

A
1   air conditioning
2   climate
3   energy bill
4   energy efficiency
5   environment
6   heat loss
7   heating
8   indoor conditions
9   insulation
10 renewable energy source
11 solar energy/power
12 thermal bridge
13 ventilation

B
1   energy efficiency
2   heat loss
3   climate
4   indoor conditions
5   heating
6   insulation
7   air conditioning
8   ventilation
9   Renewable energy sources
10 energy bills

2 PASSIVE HOUSE TECHNOLOGIES

A/B/C
(freie Lösungen)

Topic 4 Traditional and modern woodworking

1 WORKING WITH WORDS

A

1	durability	6	renewability
2	ecology	7	solidity
3	lamination	8	strong
4	length	9	structure
5	moist	10	sustainability

B

1	lamination	6	renewable
2	solid	7	ecology
3	length	8	strength
4	structural	9	durability
5	sustainability	10	moisture

2 WORKING WITH WORDS

A
(siehe Seite 19)

B
(Lösungsvorschläge)

1   sawing a piece of timber
2   clamping pieces of timber
3   feeding timber into a machine
4   pressing timber
5   programming a machine
6   operating a drill
7   planing a piece of timber
8   cutting/milling a piece of timber

Topic 5 Speech recognition

1 WORKING WITH WORDS

1	accuracy	7	improve
2	precise	8	limited
3	divide	9	standard
4	sophisticated	10	input
5	automated	11	frequent
6	analogue	12	variable

2 WORKING WITH WORDS

1   Hopefully we'll soon be able to break down the language barrier.
2   That's a great idea, but can we make it a reality?
3   Yes, of course: Google will soon unveil a new service.
4   If robots take over language services, we'll miss the human connection.
5   On the contrary: we'll be able to make meaningful connections through it.
6   It's early days for this technology.
7   Yes, but it will open up many possibilities.

3 LOOKING AT THE TEXT

(Lösungsvorschlag)

1 In order to understand new life forms, the crew of the Starship Enterprise needed a universal translator.
2 Because people speak different languages, they are less productive and connected than they could be.
3 The new Skype translator is helping to overcome language difficulties by allowing speakers of different languages to communicate in near real-time.
4 At the Code conference, Gurdeep Pall was able to show that the translator could translate between English and German without making many mistakes.
5 Two years previously, the translator had not been able to translate English to Chinese this well.
6 Gurdeep Pall believes that the translator has the potential to create new connections in education, diplomacy, families and business.
7 For 15 years, Microsoft has been researching machine translation and providing voice recognition and dictation technologies.
8 Rather than just combining speech recognition, machine translation and speech synthesis in a linear way, Microsoft has developed a neural network that can use new techniques to recognize speech.

4 LOOKING AT THE TEXT

1 e   2 b   3 a   4 f   5 c

Topic 6 Open source software

1 WORKING WITH WORDS

1	work	6	alter/modify
2	copy	7	share
3	fix	8	permit
4	modify/alter	9	agree
5	create	10	view

2 MEDIATION

(Lösungsvorschlag)

Sehr geehrter Herr …,

in unserer Schule soll neue Webdesign-Software zum Einsatz kommen. Ich plädiere dafür, dass wir Open-Source-Software verwenden, statt teure Software einzukaufen.

Das Tolle an Open-Source-Software ist, dass man hier den Source Code einsehen kann und somit mehr Kontrolle über das Produkt hat. Wir könnten dadurch selbst bestimmen, was die Software tun soll, und was nicht.

Außerdem gibt es bei Open-Source-Software weniger Bugs, denn jeder kann hier am Source Code mitarbeiten und ihn verbessern. Dadurch werden mehr Fehler gefunden und auch schneller ausgebessert, weil man hierfür nicht extra die Erlaubnis einer Firma einholen muss. Zudem kann man sich mit anderen Programmieren austauschen und sich anschauen, wie sie programmieren, und dadurch viel lernen.

Für umfangreiche, langlebige Projekte hat man bei Open-Source-Software sogar eine bessere Garantie dafür, dass die Software gut funktioniert, weil jeder ständig daran weiterarbeiten kann und man dadurch nicht von den ursprünglichen Programmierern anhängig ist.

Zu guter Letzt ist es sogar so, dass man auch bei Open-Source-Software technischen Support bekommen kann, z. B. für die Installation oder beim Troubleshooting.

Ich hoffe, die oben genannten Punkte bewegen Sie dazu, sich für Open-Source-Software zu entscheiden.

Mit freundlichen Grüßen …

3 OPEN SOURCE BUSINESS MODELS

1 crowdfunding
2 advertising-supported software
3 donationware
4 optional proprietary extensions
5 support services
6 dual-licensing
7 software as a service

Topic 7 The future of freight

1 WORKING WITH WORDS

1	warehouse	8	expend
2	ports	9	unviable
3	delivery	10	pipeline
4	efficiency	11	value
5	airport	12	environmental
6	speed	13	Bulk
7	passenger		

Load: woodchips
Mode: container ship
Origin: Helsinki
Destination: Hamburg

2 LOOKING AT THE TEXT

A
1 F, 2 T, 3 T, 4 F, 5 N, 6 T

B
(Lösungsvorschläge)

1 The aim of the SkySails system is to use the wind for ship propulsion.
2 The SkySails kite is more effective than ordinary sails because it flies in the stronger winds higher in the air.
3 Although conditions may be variable, the SkySails system can cause significant cost and emissions savings.
4 Over six years, the SkySails system has been used on different ships, including a container ship and a fishing vessel.
5 For existing ships, it is possible to retrofit a SkySails system without having to make big changes to the ship.
6 The system does not prevent the ship from moving in the normal way and carrying out its normal operations.

3 WRITING
(Lösungsvorschlag)

There are many issues to consider when discussing the future of global freight. The cost of fuel is rising and environmental protection is becoming more and more important. In this essay, I will look at these problems and show why I think this doesn't necessarily mean the end of global freight.

The first threat to global freight is rising fuel costs. Petrol and oil are very expensive, and this means that the overall costs for transporting goods keep rising. A further problem is the rise of strict environmental laws. There are more and more targets for reducing pollution and carbon emissions, which puts pressure on freight companies using lorries, ships and planes and therefore a lot of fuel.

However, I think new technology will provide solutions to these problems. There are many new ideas for more environmentally-friendly solutions to transporting freight. For example, airships are being developed that can carry large amounts of cargo using helium tanks. This means fewer emissions and the possibility to deliver goods to remote locations so that lorries can be avoided completely. Another interesting project is Skysails, which uses towing kites to harness more energy from the wind, or driverless zero-emission electric vehicles, which cut down on both cost and environmental damage.

In conclusion, I believe it is clear that rising fuel costs and trict environmental laws don't need to mean the end of global freight. The power of new technology will help freight companies to overcome these problems.

Topic 8 Cybernetics – human 2.0?

1 WORKING WITH WORDS

A
(siehe Seite 19)

1
sense (Sinn), memory (Gedächtnis), sight (Sehsinn), hearing (Gehör), strength (Stärke)

2
nerve (Nerv), brain (Gehirn), muscle (Muskel), heart (Herz), thigh (Schenkel), waist (Taille), chest (Brustkorb), joint (Gelenk)

3
implant (Implantat), processor (Prozessor), transmitter (Sender), receiver (Empfänger), electrode (Elektrode), frame (Gerüst)

B
(Lösungsvorschläge)

1 Both cybernetics and wearable robotics can help people to improve their abilities, for example to increase their strength or their hearing. The biggest difference between the two is that cybernetics involves having implants in the body, whereas wearable robotics, like a frame to help you lift things, are temporary and easy to remove.

2 Cybernetics can help people to improve their hearing. One example would be the use of cochlear implants which are put into a person's ear. An external microphone picks up sounds and a transmitter then sends the signals to the device so that the person can hear better. Wearable robotics can be used to help people lift things. An exoskeleton, for example, can be attached to the wearer's waist and be used to increase strength.

2 ROBOTIC EXOSKELETON
(freie Lösung)

Topic 9 Biometric security technology

1 WORD FIELDS

1 clone, replicate, fake, forge
2 alive, living, in real life
3 identification, recognition, analysis, identify

2 WORKING WITH WORDS

1	characteristics	6	rhythm
2	Fingerprint	7	enter
3	pattern	8	signature
4	secure	9	complexity
5	measure	10	identification

3 LOOKING AT THE TEXT

1	f	3	e	5	a
2	b	4	g	6	d

4 WORD FAMILIES

1	universal	9	authentic
2	permanent	10	authentication
3	measure	11	suitable
4	measurable	12	suitability
5	performance	13	different
6	accept	14	difference
7	acceptability	15	accurate
8	circumvention	16	imitation

Topic 10 Electric vehicles

1 ANNOTATING A DIAGRAM
(freie Lösung)

2 WORKING WITH WORDS
(Lösungsvorschlag)

1 Hybrid electric vehicles are vehicles that have a fuel tank and a battery bank. They run on petrol and electricity.
2 Electric propulsion uses electricity to power or propel a motor.
3 An internal combustion engine is a heat engine where fuel combusts to provide power.

4 Fuel economy describes the relationship between the distance a vehicle travels and the amount of fuel it consumes.

5 Acceleration is when a vehicle speeds up.

6 Performance describes how well a vehicle functions.

7 The drivetrain is the part of a vehicle that gives the wheels power.

3 COMPARING HEV SYSTEMS
(Lösungsvorschlag)

Diagram number one shows a parallel hybrid and diagram two is a series hybrid. Both of these hybrids combine a combustion engine with an electric motor, but in different ways. The engine and electric motor in a parallel hybrid are both attached to the wheels. This means they can power the vehicle together or individually. The electric motor can be used for city driving and the engine when the vehicle is on the motorway, for example. In contrast, the engine in a series hybrid isn't connected to the drivetrain. The engine is used to run a generator to generate electricity for the electric motor. This gives the vehicle an extended range with a small and fuel-efficient engine, and it means that the electric vehicle can go everywhere a petrol-driven car can go without running out of power.

Topic 11 Keeping track of food

1 WORKING WITH WORDS

A

1	o	6	f	11	d
2	l	7	i	12	g
3	a	8	j	13	h
4	k	9	c	14	e
5	m	10	n	15	b

B

1 **1** storage capacity; **2** tag
2 **1** on-board; **2** memory
3 **1** range; **2** track
4 **1** idle; **2** transmitting
5 **1** conserve; **2** power source
6 **1** detects; **2** field

2 LOOKING AT THE TEXT
(Lösungsvorschläge)

1 What is the Internet of Things?
2 How does data get on to the Internet?
3 Why is the Internet of Things needed?
4 What other technologies are needed for the Internet of Things?
5 When will the Internet of Things happen?

3 WRITING A COMMENT
(Lösungsvorschlag)

The topic of the Internet of Things is very interesting. It promises to make life more convenient, but there are a lot of different things to take into consideration. I will now look at the two sides of the argument.

The Internet of Things is supposed to make our life easier. In my view, some things may be useful. A pacemaker that can communicate with the doctor's equipment and automatically say when there is a problem, for example, could save lives. Cars that communicate with each other and drive themselves may also have some benefits: lower numbers of cars on the road, for example, and less pollution. On the other hand, these things can be dangerous if there is a system problem or a hacker attacks the system. If a driverless car has a system failure, there would be huge problems. Even smaller devices are not secure. For example, recently it was in the news that TVs with voice recognition, where you can tell your TV what to do orally, always have the microphones on, so they always hear what you say. If the wrong person hacks into this system, they can find out a lot of personal information.

To sum up, I think that the Internet of Things is a good idea, but I have concerns about safety and privacy.

Topic 12 3D printing

1 WORKING WITH WORDS

1	assemble	8	moving
2	capabilities	9	slice
3	finish	10	smooth
4	layer	11	solid
5	hinge	12	item
6	replace	13	tiny
7	design	14	object

2 LOOKING AT THE TEXT

1–3	tank, UV light, photoreactive
4	movable platform
5 + 6	layers, polymer
7–10	wire, filament, spool, print head
11 + 12	metal, heat
13–15	fuse/sinter, glass, powder

3 3D PRINTING SOLUTIONS
(Lösungsvorschläge)

1 Liquids and powders are a problem in zero gravity because they float around. That would be very dangerous in a spacecraft or on the ISS. I would use fused deposition modelling because the filament or wire is easy to control even without gravity.

2 Fused deposition modelling and selective laser sintering are both possible. I would use selective laser sintering because a wider range of metals can be used. Stereolithography is not suitable because it can only be used with polymers.

3 All of the 3D printing techniques could be used. However, in an office it is important to use a clean technique that does not leave powder or liquid behind, so I would choose fused deposition modelling. This is also a simple type of 3D printer that is easy to maintain.

TOPIC 4, EXERCISE 2A, WORD SQUARE (WB, p. 71)

T	O	R	O	T	A	T	E	D	E	A	T
S	A	W	N	P	R	E	R	I	N	T	P
C	S	A	D	A	P	R	E	S	S	E	R
T	E	F	A	C	R	A	D	S	T	R	O
E	A	E	R	K	I	M	I	L	L	E	G
S	R	E	E	A	N	I	K	A	S	S	R
T	H	D	F	G	C	L	A	M	P	D	A
E	A	R	F	E	I	E	H	O	A	T	M
P	L	A	N	E	R	D	R	Y	L	I	E
R	I	P	A	N	A	R	A	T	L	L	R
O	N	O	P	E	R	A	T	E	E	T	A
C	U	T	E	T	R	A	N	S	F	E	R

TOPIC 8, EXERCISE 1A, WORD SQUARE (WB, p. 78)

S	A	M	E	M	O	R	Y	A	D	O	P	B	R
E	T	R	A	N	S	M	I	T	T	E	R	R	E
N	M	E	L	A	N	W	Q	U	A	N	O	A	S
S	U	C	P	W	E	J	O	I	N	T	C	I	I
E	S	E	W	A	E	E	I	K	E	R	E	N	G
R	C	I	A	I	D	T	B	R	S	I	S	Y	H
S	L	V	R	S	I	R	A	A	A	F	S	U	T
E	E	E	N	T	E	L	E	C	T	R	O	D	E
L	T	R	O	A	S	A	R	H	R	A	R	T	B
N	I	M	P	L	A	N	T	E	H	M	A	H	R
O	L	D	R	A	C	U	T	S	I	E	R	I	A
S	T	R	E	N	G	T	H	T	E	R	G	G	N
A	R	I	A	S	A	N	E	R	V	E	N	H	A
H	E	A	R	T	H	E	A	R	I	N	G	A	W

Audioscripts

Unit 1, Exercise 7B

Desirée Hi Patrick.

Patrick Hi Desirée. I am calling from my car. What are you doing at the moment?

Desirée I'm reading the latest report about us in the newspaper.

Patrick What story is the press making up now?

Desirée That you're dating another woman.

Patrick These people are going too far. Are they trying to split us up?

Desirée I suppose they are only doing their job. Oh, no! Two reporters are walking up the path to the front door.

Patrick Don't worry, darling. I'm driving into your street right now. I can see them. Hey, you!

Unit 2, Exercise 6

1

Interviewer Good morning, Jane. Thanks for agreeing to talk to our listeners about keeping fit. You do aerobics, I believe?

Jane That's right. As far as I'm concerned, aerobics is one of the best ways to stay healthy. It strengthens the heart and the lungs and it's also a great way to reduce stress. It's exactly the right thing for me after a long day at work.

Interviewer Yes. I can imagine that all those powerful moves help to get rid of stress. How often do you do aerobics?

Jane I go to a class once a week, but I also do aerobics at home. I just put on some music and do the moves.

Interviewer What would you say to anyone thinking about doing aerobics as a way to keep fit?

Jane It's a fun way to keep fit and it's not too expensive. You don't really need any special clothes and once you've paid for the class, all you have to do is get there on time, join in and have fun.

Interviewer So what you're saying is that doing aerobics offers quite a few health benefits. It's good for the heart and the lungs and the muscles. And it helps you get rid of stress. It's fun and it's not expensive so, if you're thinking of doing something to keep fit, why not do as Jane does, join an aerobics class and have fun!

2

Interviewer I've come to the local swimming pool where I'm talking to Will about swimming as a way to keep fit. Good evening, Will. Thanks for your time.

Will No problem.

Interviewer To begin with, why have you chosen swimming as a way to keep fit?

Will Well, you exercise every bit of your body and it's a great work-out. It's also a very relaxing activity, so it helps me to sleep well. The main reason why I go swimming, though, is to get slim and stay slim. I gave up sport when I left college and then I started to get fat. I've lost two kilos since I started swimming regularly.

Interviewer That sounds great, Will. It's a good work-out and helps you sleep and you're losing weight, too.

Will That's right. I'd definitely recommend swimming as a good way to keep fit. You don't have to have a great body to go swimming. People of all shapes and sizes go swimming.

Interviewer Thanks, Will. Just to go over what you said: when you swim, you exercise every part of your body. Swimming helps you relax, so you can sleep well and it also helps you lose weight. So, all you listeners, if you feel you need any of these benefits, it doesn't matter what you look like, get your swimming gear on and jump in!

3

Interviewer The last person I'm talking to today is Lily. She's just finished an exciting game of volleyball. Hi, Lily. How was the game?

Lily My team didn't win, but everyone had a lot of fun. That's one of the good things about volleyball. Even if you lose a game, you still feel great afterwards.

Interviewer Anything that gives you a good feeling must be good for your health. What about the other health benefits of playing volleyball?

Lily Well, it certainly burns calories. That's not why I took up volleyball, though. I've never been overweight. No, when I started college, I wanted to get to know people so I looked for a team sport. The people in the volleyball team here at college were really nice, so I joined the club.

Interviewer Team sports certainly are a good way to get to know people.

Lily Definitely, every team sport helps you make friends. You're working together to get the best result and that makes you feel good, too.

Interviewer And that's another health benefit, eh? Well, listeners, what about volleyball as a way to keep fit? It's a lot of fun, it makes you feel great and it burns up calories. It's a team sport and, as Lily said, team sports help you make friends, and working together with them for a good result keeps you healthy, too. Thanks, Lily.

Unit 3, Exercise 4

Oh, dear. I'm not sure which of these three phones to choose. I can see that the Universe is bigger than the NeatPhone and the Bright is the biggest of all three, but I'll have to think some more.

How heavy are they? The NeatPhone is lighter than the two other phones. The Universe is not as heavy as the Bright. The Bright is heavier than the other two.

What does it say here about the battery life? The battery life of the NeatPhone is not as long as the battery life of the Bright. It looks as if the batteries of the Universe last longest.

What about the price? Well, the Bright is the cheapest of the phones. The NeatPhone is more expensive than the Bright and the Universe is the most expensive of them all.

Oh, I don't know which of these three phones is best. Choosing a phone is one of the most difficult things to do in life. Hmmm. I think I'll buy the NeatPhone. It's the lightest and it looks the nicest. Yes. It's the NeatPhone. That's the one I'll buy.

Unit 5, Exercise 5

Catherine	Hello?
Margaret	Oh, hello. Am I speaking to Catherine Seale?
Catherine	Yes, that's right. Who's speaking, please?
Margaret	It's Margaret Green. Your son Christopher and my son Jamie are in the same class at school.
Catherine	Ah, yes I remember! I think Jamie was at our house a few weeks ago. If you're trying to reach Christopher, please try him on his mobile because my husband and I are on holiday in France at the moment.
Margaret	In France! Oh dear! I thought you were here in London. Well, I think I under-stand better what's happening now because I've just brought Jamie to your house for the party and …
Catherine	Party! What party? I told him not to have any parties!
Margaret	Well, there's certainly one going on in your house at the moment. I'm in my car outside and I think it's out of control. There are young people everywhere, some are drunk and vomiting in the front garden and I think I can see someone on the roof.
Catherine	On the roof! That can't be true! Oh my god, what's happening?

Margaret	I think the boy on the roof is trying to open the skylight. I think he's trying to break in. It doesn't look good here, Catherine. There's very loud music and from what I can see they're all dancing wildly in the front room.
Catherine	On my new carpet! They'll trash it! Can't you stop them somehow?
Margaret	I'm not sure but can you hear that siren?
Catherine	Siren? You mean the police siren?
Margaret	Yes, the riot police are here now and they're breaking up all the people blocking the street and in the front garden.
Catherine	The riot police are breaking up the people blocking the street! How many are there outside the house?
Margaret	I would say hundreds. I'm so sorry to tell you all this but I think they must be gatecrashers because Jamie said Christopher only invited 60 people and was going to have a bouncer to make sure nobody else got in.
Catherine	I just don't believe this! Is my son Christopher there?
Margaret	I can't see him. He must be inside but I don't want to go in there with all those drunken revellers. Anyway, the riot police have stopped the people wrecking the front garden now.
Catherine	My husband has been listening and we're getting the first flight back to London! Thanks for letting me know, Margaret.
Margaret	Don't mention it and have a nice flight!

Unit 6, Exercise 3B

We hope you're enjoying your flight with High Sky Air Travel. In a few moments, you will have the chance to take advantage of our super in-flight perfume and cosmetics prices, which are up to 40% cheaper than on the high street. Yes, you heard it right! As a passenger on a High Sky flight you have the chance to buy top brand perfume and cosmetics up to 40% cheaper! These prices are valid until just before we land in London, so this is a real chance for you to save money. For example, why not buy a 50 ml bottle of a top brand perfume for just £40 and save £15 pounds on high street prices? Or a 75 ml top brand deodorant stick for men for just £12 compared to £20 in your local store? These are just two examples of our unbelievable offers. Pay by card or cash in pounds or euros when our cabin crew come by and ask them to show you what other great deals we have for you.

Unit 7, Exercise 6

Officer	Well, Carrie, let's start with some personal details, shall we?

Carrie	Fine, yes.
Officer	So first, can I have your family name?
Carrie	It's Keighley.
Officer	Could you spell that for me, please?
Carrie	Yes. It's K-e-i-g-h-l-e-y.
Officer	Right, and your first name? What is Carrie short for?
Carrie	Carole – with an 'e' on the end. And my middle name is Elisabeth. That's spelt with an 's', not a 'z', by the way.
Officer	So your given names are Carole – C-a-r-o-l-e – Elisabeth – E-l-i-s-a-b-e-t-h.
Carrie	That's right.
Officer	And what age are you now?
Carrie	I'm 17 now. My birthday was last month. The 13th of October.
Officer	The 30th of October?
Carrie	No, the 13th.
Officer	Thanks, so that gives me your date of birth … And now can I make a note of your home address, please?
Carrie	Yes, it's 7 Bow Road, Wendcot.
Officer	OK, so that's 7 Bow Road, Wendcot. And the post code?
Carrie	It's AL7 8NB.
Officer	AL7 8NB. Good, and now your phone number?
Carrie	I'll give you my mobile, all right?
Officer	That's fine.
Carrie	It's oh-double-seven-six-five …
Officer	Oh-double-seven-six-five …
Carrie	One-double-eight-three-double-nine.
Officer	Double-one-eight-three-double-nine.
Carrie	No, sorry. That's one-double-eight-three-double-nine.
Officer	Oh, right. Good. Now, let's talk about your situation at home …

Unit 8, Exercise 1

8

Dialogue 1

Advisor	Good morning, Meera.
Meera	Good morning.
Advisor	Please take a seat.
Meera	Thanks.
Advisor	I'm very glad you've come, Meera, because it's a good idea to start planning your career early, and 16 is a good age to start. The first thing I'm going to do is ask you a few questions to find out what sort of person you are. Alright?

Meera	Yes, fine.
Advisor	What's your dream job?
Meera	Dream job … er … I'm not sure, really. I don't really know.
Advisor	Don't worry. Not many people can answer that question. What activities do you do outside school in your free time?
Meera	Well, I signed up for our school's community service group and we visit people who need some help. For example, there are mothers with young children who need help at home, sometimes just holding the baby or playing with the toddlers. And then there's an old man near the school who needs a bit of shopping done. That kind of thing.
Advisor	That's very helpful information, Meera. Now what about your subjects at school? Which ones do you like most?
Meera	Well, I love art! I won the art prize last year for a painting I did and it's still up on the wall in the entrance to our school as you come in. And I like English, of course. I like to read stories about what life is like for young people in other countries. That sort of thing. Oh, and I forgot sport. I like basketball and football, too.
Advisor	And are there any subjects you don't like?
Meera	Chemistry! I really don't know why we do it. Biology is hard work, too.
Advisor	Well, I'm getting a picture of you now, Meera. Do you have any work experience?
Meera	No, not really.
Advisor	Not helping out in a shop, giving out leaflets, baby-sitting or anything like that?
Meera	Oh, yes baby-sitting, of course! That's not work. That's fun!
Advisor	And do you get paid for it?
Meera	Oh, yes. I'm always being asked by friends and family. Last month I made almost a hundred pounds!
Advisor	Well, I think I have a picture of you now, Meera. I think you might like a job looking after people, young or old, so I think you should do a work placement in a kindergarten, an old people's home or a hospital and then come back to me.
Meera	A kindergarten would be nice.
Advisor	Here's a list of addresses to contact … *(fade)*

Dialogue 2

Advisor	Good morning, Christopher.
Christopher	Hi.
Advisor	Please take a seat.
Christopher	Thanks.

Advisor	I'm glad you've come to see me, Christopher, because I think 17 is a good time to think about planning your future.
Christopher	Look, to be honest I'm here because everybody in my year has to see a careers advisor when they're 17. I already know what I want to do and on my 18th birthday I'm going to walk out of school and do it.
Advisor	Before your exams in May?
Christopher	Yes. My 18th birthday's in March, so I can leave on the day I'm 18.
Advisor	That's a big decision to make, Christopher. You're doing well at school. I can see that from your good results. Do you really dislike school that much?
Christopher	It's meaningless. I see my friends there but I'm basically just wasting my time.
Advisor	So you already know what your dream job is?
Christopher	Yes, I'm going to be a top DJ and my ambition is to be a DJ headliner at the Ultra Music Festival in Miami. I don't need school for that, do I?
Advisor	I see. How much do you know about the job?
Christopher	Well, in my free time I'm a DJ. And in the holidays I had a guest DJ residency at Your Mum's House. It was great!
Advisor	And Your Mum's House is the name of a nightclub?
Christopher	Yes, it's a number one club. I've played there and they want me back.
Advisor	Well, I can see you know a lot about music and that you're very ambitious, but I still have some questions I'd like to ask you. Is that alright?
Christopher	Fire away.
Advisor	What are your favourite subjects at school?
Christopher	None.
Advisor	Is there absolutely nothing you like at school?
Christopher	The only thing I like doing there is sport because I want to keep fit. A DJ has to look good and I like to work out. Once we did some body-building in sport and that was good.
Advisor	OK, sport and body-building and you don't like anything else at school?
Christopher	No, nothing, and of all the things I don't like, history's the subject I hate most of all.
Advisor	Alright, and apart from DJ'ing do you have any other work experience?

Christopher	I had a Saturday job in a shop selling jeans. It was alright but nothing special. And I worked in a tattoo studio. That was good and I got some cool tattoos.
Advisor	Well, I think I have a good picture of you now, Christopher.
Christopher	Good. Can I go now?
Advisor	Yes, of course, I don't want to keep you here against your will, but have you ever thought about learning a musical instrument or studying music? As you spend all your free time working with music, it would help you in your career – but you'd need to stay on at school and take your exams to study music.
Christopher	Hm, I suppose studying music could be helpful. I'll think about it …

Unit 9, Exercise 5

Presenter	Welcome to *Behind the News*. Well, US immigration is a hot political topic again, so let's take a look at it. To help us, Professor David Newman is going to talk us through the facts and figures. Well now, Professor Newman, America is a country of immigrants, isn't it? So are today's immigration numbers really so dramatic?
Newman	Well, yes and no. Way back, over a century ago, the statistics were quite similar to the figures today, so the situation now isn't new. But in between, something different happened. You see, from the early 1900s, there was a long, long fall in immigration that continued till around 1970. By that time, immigrant numbers were low – around 9.6 million out of a population of just over 200 million. That meant that the immigrant share of the population was only about 5%.
Presenter	So what's happened since then?
Newman	Well, since then, the figures have risen quite rapidly. By 1980, the number of immigrants was around 6% of the population. That was a total of 14.1 million people. And the trend continued. By 1990, the immigrant population had reached 19.8 million out of a total of just under 250 million. As a percentage, that was about 8% of the total. Then by the start of this century, in the year 2000, we see another big jump to 11% of the total population. By that time, there were 31.1 million immigrants in America.
Presenter	And more recently?
Newman	Well, in 2012, the total population was approximately 313.7 million. At the same time, the immigrant population reached 40.8 million. That was around 13% of

the whole US population. This took US immigration back to the levels that used to arrive in America around a century ago. And the trend is still rising today.

Unit 10, Exercise 4

In this podcast we'll hear how a charity set up by a survivor of the 2004 Boxing Day tsunami has provided emergency relief to people whose lives were destroyed.

Clare Allen and her daughter Daisy were on holiday in Sri Lanka when the tsunami struck. Luckily, the huge waves stopped just short of her hotel and her daughter, who had been on the beach, was found safe. The tsunami killed 40,000 people in Sri Lanka and left over a million homeless, so emergency help was desperately needed. After her miraculous escape, Clare decided to set up a charity, which she called *Rebuilding Sri Lanka*, and since then the charity has built 300 homes, a special needs school, two schools for young children, five libraries and an English language centre, to name just a few of its achievements.

One of its many projects is called 'Books and Buns', meaning education and food for children of school age. In many parts of Sri Lanka the school buildings have not been improved or repaired for decades and children who wish to pass their school-leaving exams have to pay for extra lessons and spend about £2,000 on school books. This makes it impossible for poor children to get a good education, so *Rebuilding Sri Lanka* has built modern libraries with new and up-to-date school books. Its largest library has over 2,700 members and every Saturday more than 200 books are borrowed from it.

Poor children often walk long distances to school and arrive tired and hungry, so *Rebuilding Sri Lanka* gives meals to over 5,000 schoolchildren a day. The result is a 23% increase in school attendance.

Its other projects include finding jobs for the unemployed, supporting hospitals with medical supplies and equipment and a Children's Resource Centre where traumatized children, some of whom have lost one or both parents, can receive counselling.

Rebuilding Sri Lanka is proud of the fact that its website designers, accountants and fundraisers all work for free, meaning that only 5% of the money it collects is spent on administration. 95% of donations are therefore used to help people in need.

Unit 11, Exercise 4

So now we can look back over the four years since the Gumutindo Coffee Cooperative was formed, and we can see that things have gone really well – after a slow start.

In the first half of Year 1, sales rose gradually from zero to around 500 kilos a month. They then remained unchanged at that level for the rest of Year 1. In Year 2, the change to organic production took place, and this meant a rapid fall to zero again for a short time at the end of the first half. However, organic sales then took off well in the second half, and they climbed rapidly to 1,000 kilos a month by the end of the year. In Year 3, there was a steady increase in sales to 1,500 kilos a

month by the end of the first half. This was at the same time as processed coffee production began – the now-famous Gumutindo Gold Brand. This soon affected sales of unprocessed coffee, and so there was only a slight further increase to 1,600 kilos by the end of Year 3. And this year, Gold Brand sales have really taken off. Because of this, sales of unprocessed beans declined steadily to 1,400 kilos a month in the first half, and since then, in the second half, there has been a sharp further decrease to just 800 kilos per month.

Now, Gold Brand has been a huge success story, as we all know, so let's now take a look at sales of this product.

Unit 12, Exercise 3

Carlos	Hello? Can you see me?
Peter	Yes, I can see you just fine. Hello there. And who am I speaking to?
Carlos	My name's Carlos Branco.
Peter	Well, hi. And I'm Peter North. Nice to meet you.
Carlos	And it's good to meet you too, Mr North. Thank you for agreeing to talk to me like this on Skype.
Peter	Oh, please just call me Peter. Anyway, I'm only too happy to try this Skype idea. It's nice to see a new face – especially a young one! Now how do you want to do this?
Carlos	Maybe we should tell each other a little about ourselves. Er … would you like to start?
Peter	Sure. Well, I'm Peter North, as I said, and I turned 83 years old yesterday.
Carlos	Wow! Happy birthday! And have you been at Windsor Park for long?
Peter	For about two years. Until then, I lived alone for many years, but it was getting hard to look after everything.
Carlos	Do you have any family?
Peter	Well, sadly my wife Lucy died twelve years ago.
Carlos	I'm sorry to hear that.
Peter	But I have three children – two sons and a daughter.
Carlos	And do you have any grandchildren?
Peter	Yes, six! All my children have children of their own.
Carlos	Fantastic! And what sort of ages are they?
Peter	They go all the way down from 18 to just two.
Carlos	They must be fun!
Peter	They are. And you know what? All three families came yesterday to take me out for a birthday party at a really nice restaurant. It was a big surprise. I couldn't believe my eyes when they all came through the door!

Carlos Wow! A very special day! But tell me, what do you usually do from day to day at Windsor Park? Do you have any special interests?

Peter Oh, yes, there are lots of things you can do here. For example, I go to an art class every Wednesday. I listen to a lot of music, too – mostly jazz. And when they organize day trips for the residents, I always try to join them. It's nice here, but you have to get out when you can.

Unit 13, Exercise 4

Host Good evening and welcome to our live radio show *Across the country*. Our topic this evening is surveillance cameras. We've all noticed them and some of us feel safer when we see them but others certainly don't. It's estimated that there are almost six million CCTV cameras across the UK and new cameras are being installed every day, so do we just need to accept them or is now the time to do something before it's too late? Our studio guests are Detective Inspector John Langton, journalist Sally Herald, Student's Union representative Megan O'Hara and actor Johnny Pitt. We'll also be reading out your emails, texts and tweets to hear your views. Let's start off the discussion with Detective Inspector Langton. How do the police see surveillance cameras?

Inspector The British public have the right to feel safe wherever they are, day and night, seven days a week, 52 weeks a year and we, as the nation's police force, have to make sure this happens. That's why we use everything possible to do our job. That includes surveillance cameras. Whether it's the student whose mobile is stolen, the old lady who has her handbag taken or the terrorist who leaves a bomb in a public place – we need to act fast and surveillance cameras often give us the information we need. I believe they help to make the UK a safer place.

Host Sally Herald, as a journalist, do you share the police's opinion?

Herald Well, I wouldn't be a journalist if I did! There's some truth in what he says, of course, but that's not the whole story. We, in the UK, have become camera-mad! We have cameras in places we don't expect them and certainly don't need them! The whole country's camera-crazy but I think we just don't notice them anymore.

Host And what are these places where we don't expect or need them?

Herald Schools and hospitals, for example. These places are full of people with eyes in their heads! Why do we need cameras?

Host Well, we've heard two very opposing views now, so Johnny Pitt, you spend a lot of time in front of cameras. Do you also like them to watch you in the street when you're going about your daily business?

Pitt Well, I guess I find it normal to see cameras everywhere. The world is a dangerous place and I think that if people know there's a good chance that there's a camera recording them, they'll think twice before breaking the law. Privacy is of course important but I'm willing to lose some of it to stay safe if it reduces crime.

Host Megan O'Hara, you represent the UK's student community. What do you think about the importance of personal safety and privacy?

O'Hara I want safety *and* privacy. I don't agree that it's a question of one or the other. There was personal safety before we had cameras everywhere and now we have more and more cameras and less and less personal safety. As for privacy, we can forget it! Not only do we have surveillance cameras recording our every move, whistleblowers now tell us that hackers can secretly turn on our mobile phone cameras, so how do we know the police aren't doing this, as well? I also don't agree with Johnny Pitt that cameras will make people think twice before breaking the law. Cameras may help the police *after* a crime but they don't *stop* crimes.

Host Would you like to comment on that Detective Inspector Langton?

Inspector The police don't break the law, Ms O'Hara! We defend it and we use all legal methods to protect citizens of this country, no more and no less.

O'Hara Oh really! It didn't look like that at our last student demonstration when the police …

Host Let's stick to the point, please. Sally Herald, do you agree that cameras can prevent crimes?

Herald Well, I certainly don't agree with Johnny Pitt on that point. We all remember that picture of him punching a photographer outside his hotel, so I don't think he thinks twice before breaking the law!

Pitt That was self-defence! The guy was in my way and wouldn't move. It just looked like a punch!

Herald That's not what the doctor said at the hospital! I interviewed him personally and he said he thought the photographer had been hit by a boxer. I'm sure you were making a boxing movie at the time …

Host	I think it's time to hear our listeners' comments. We have a tweet from …

 Unit 14, Exercise 3

Jenny Wade	I think it's crazy to take any more fossil fuels out of the ground when we know that climate change is getting out of control. Now, what we need to do is to invest everything in renewable forms of energy. That way, we'll have a chance of saving the world for our children and grandchildren.
Stella King	I'm really worried about the noise, with big trucks going along our narrow roads at all hours, day and night. And think how dangerous it will be for us all – especially for our children. We mustn't allow this development to take place.
Lyn Benson	It probably won't be easy for the community for a while, that's for sure. But they're promising to put a lot of money into the community in return, and that will do some real good for all of us far into the future.
Brian Fox	I'm old enough to remember times when the lights went out, and it wasn't nice. We've already closed down a lot of the old coal-fired power stations, and it'll be years before renewables can replace them. And gas is a lot cleaner than coal, so we should use that to keep the lights on for the next 20 years.
Alan Smith	Why should we support this fracking project? It doesn't make any sense, does it? I mean, this is the sort of thing that'll give a lot more money to people who already have a lot of money. And what do we local people get in return? Nothing – nothing but trouble!
Bob Lowe	I think we should welcome this development even if it means accepting some noise and a bit of a hard time for a few months. Remember: after those few months, production will continue year after year without any more problems. That seems all right to me – especially as I may be able to get a job!

 Unit 15, Exercise 5A

So you're hungry, but let's say you've only got £10 to spend. What will you buy – fast food or fresh food to cook for yourselves?

Well, if you go to your local fast-food restaurant, it's all very simple. You'll be able to get two burgers that cost £2.40 each for a total of £4.80. With those, of course, you'll want two portions of French fries and they'll cost you another £3.20. After that, well, you need something to drink and two medium colas will cost £1.80. Is there enough for any extras – fruit yogurts, perhaps? Well,

no, because you've already spent £9.80 on your rather basic dinner for two.

Now, if you go to the supermarket, you'll get more for your money. For two portions of chicken, you'll need to pay £3.10. Half a kilo of potatoes will be yours for just 60 pence. Then allow £3.80 for some healthy salad vegetables. You can get some fruit, too, for another £1.20. And finally, you can get a litre of milk for just 90 pence. Total: £9.60 and you've got yourselves a good, healthy dinner for two that won't leave you hungry in the middle of the night!

 Unit 15, Exercise 5B

So why does anyone choose fast food? Well, they might prefer to eat fast food for various reasons. First of all, some people just love this sort of food. After all, these big fast-food chains do a lot of research on creating food that's tasty – food that people want to come back for again and again. Secondly, there are also lots of people who really don't like cooking very much. It's too much of a chore, and they're more interested in their work or in other things. Thirdly, these days there are other people who really don't know how to cook. They just never learned, perhaps because their own parents were too busy to teach them. And finally, of course, fast food is what it says it is: fast. In today's busy world, a lot of people have to rush round all the time – perhaps between two different jobs, for example. For them, fast food just takes less time and trouble than a home-cooked meal.

 Unit 15, Exercise 5C

So just how much time and trouble do these different types of meal take? Well, let's think about your local fast-food restaurant first. Let's say going there and back takes 15 minutes. Then when you're there, you have to order what you want and then wait for a short time, so let's say ordering takes five minutes. And after that, there's just the eating, and it isn't a very big meal, is it? So let's say eating takes another 15 minutes. That's a total of 35 minutes and you're all done.

But now what about the home-cooked meal? Well first you've got to go and get everything from the shop and then get home again. So let's say shopping takes 45 minutes. Then there's preparing the food – washing the vegetables, cooking and so on. So let's allow another 45 minutes for preparing. Now comes the good bit – eating! Well, you've got quite a big meal, so that should take another 20 minutes. Then, finally, there's washing up and tidying up to do after that. Not so nice, but very important. And let's allow 15 minutes for that. That's a total of 125 minutes all together. Over two hours in other words!

 Unit 16, Exercise 4

Mark Moro	Now let's open the debate about driverless cars to our studio audience. First, please, the lady in the green jacket.
Sylvia Ray	Thank you. I'm Sylvia Ray and I'm an A & E nurse. Every day I see the horrible results of road accidents – accidents

usually caused by human error. So I'm in favour of this new technology. It seems to me that driverless cars have the potential to cut the number of deaths and injuries on the roads. We don't have as many emergency service staff and doctors and nurses as we need, and you know what? Thanks to driverless cars, we'll now be released to handle more of the other medical problems we're trained to deal with.

Mark Moro   Thank you. All right, well now let's hear from the man in the grey suit.

Ben Miller   I'm Ben Miller. I'm the Director of Right Road Construction and, as you might expect, I think driverless cars are a terrible idea! If they can really drive very close together, that means we'll never need to build any more roads. That'll cut the need for the work my organization does – road construction. The only thing anyone will want us for is to repair the roads and bridges we've already got. Thinking about the whole road construction industry, that'll cost lots of jobs. I don't want to see that.

Mark Moro   Thank you. So we've now had one view in favour and one view very much against driverless cars. Now the young lady in the yellow blouse.

Julie North   Thank you. Well, I'm Julie North and I'm a car insurance salesperson, and from a personal point of view I'm against driverless cars. If they really and truly mean a much higher level of safety, then that will bring down the amount drivers have to pay for their car insurance. And that can only mean one thing: many of the people selling car insurance like me will have to start again – maybe training to sell other sorts of insurance instead.

Mark Moro   Thank you. Well, I can see that would be a problem for some people, though a lot more people would be very happy to see the cost of driving come down like that. All right, let's have one more opinion now. The man in the blue jacket, please.

Peter Hill   I'm Peter Hill. I'm a city planning officer, and I have to say that I'm very much in favour of this new technology. I want our cities to work more efficiently, and one of the really inefficient things is the way traffic moves – or doesn't move. A lot of the time, cars are parked on roads or in great big car parks. Now driverless cars will be shared by lots of people, and so that problem will mostly disappear because these cars won't need to be parked for long. As soon as one person has driven into the city centre, for example, the car can be called to someone else. It'll drive straight there, pick up the next person and drive to the next place.

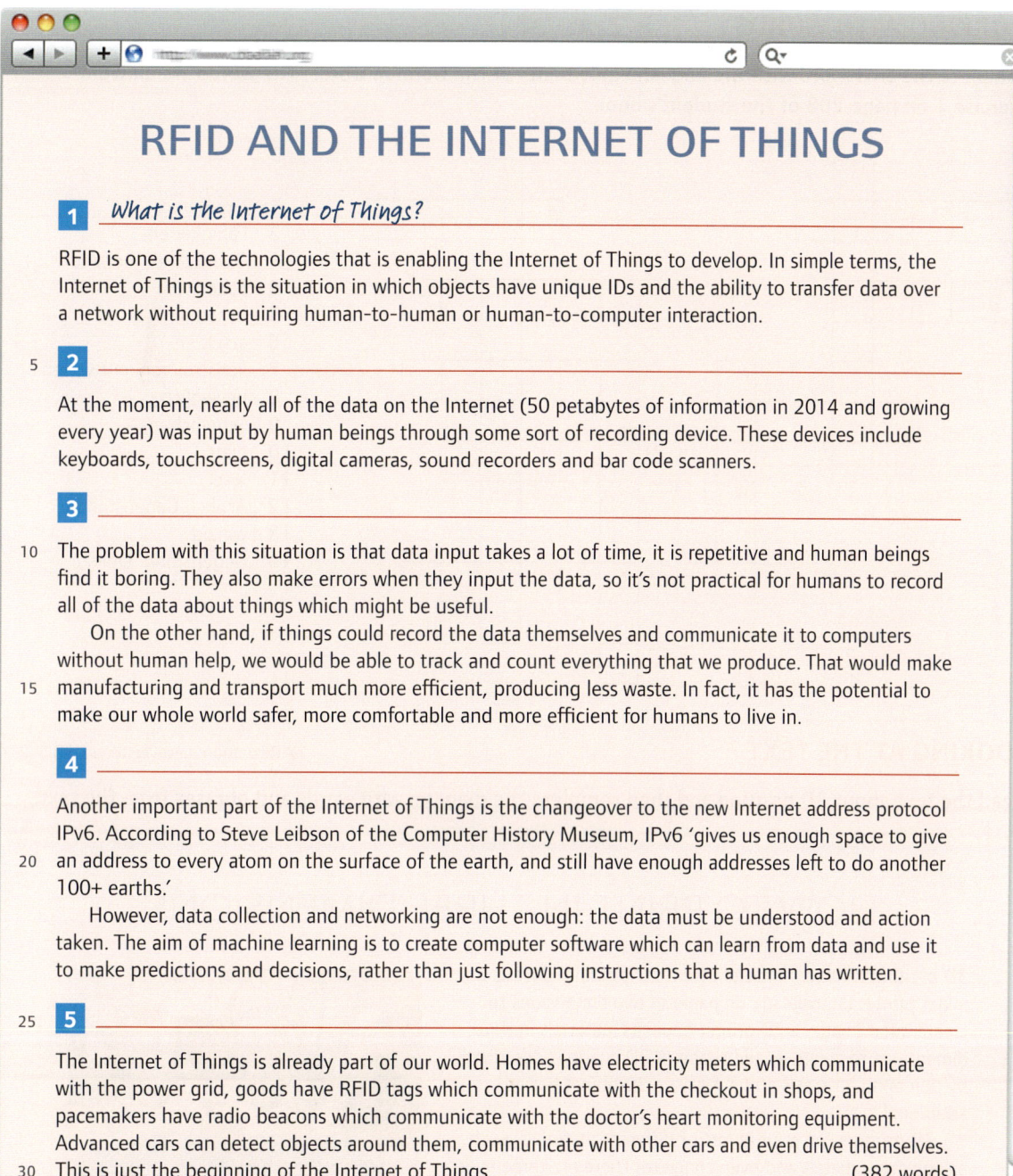

RFID AND THE INTERNET OF THINGS

1 *What is the Internet of Things?*

RFID is one of the technologies that is enabling the Internet of Things to develop. In simple terms, the Internet of Things is the situation in which objects have unique IDs and the ability to transfer data over a network without requiring human-to-human or human-to-computer interaction.

5 **2**

At the moment, nearly all of the data on the Internet (50 petabytes of information in 2014 and growing every year) was input by human beings through some sort of recording device. These devices include keyboards, touchscreens, digital cameras, sound recorders and bar code scanners.

3

10 The problem with this situation is that data input takes a lot of time, it is repetitive and human beings find it boring. They also make errors when they input the data, so it's not practical for humans to record all of the data about things which might be useful.

On the other hand, if things could record the data themselves and communicate it to computers without human help, we would be able to track and count everything that we produce. That would make
15 manufacturing and transport much more efficient, producing less waste. In fact, it has the potential to make our whole world safer, more comfortable and more efficient for humans to live in.

4

Another important part of the Internet of Things is the changeover to the new Internet address protocol IPv6. According to Steve Leibson of the Computer History Museum, IPv6 'gives us enough space to give
20 an address to every atom on the surface of the earth, and still have enough addresses left to do another 100+ earths.'

However, data collection and networking are not enough: the data must be understood and action taken. The aim of machine learning is to create computer software which can learn from data and use it to make predictions and decisions, rather than just following instructions that a human has written.

25 **5**

The Internet of Things is already part of our world. Homes have electricity meters which communicate with the power grid, goods have RFID tags which communicate with the checkout in shops, and pacemakers have radio beacons which communicate with the doctor's heart monitoring equipment. Advanced cars can detect objects around them, communicate with other cars and even drive themselves.
30 This is just the beginning of the Internet of Things. (382 words)

---

3 **WRITING A COMMENT** → Eine Stellungnahme schreiben, SB S. 234

One of your friends read the article *RFID and the Internet of Things* in exercise 2 and wrote: 'The Internet of Things will be a hacker's dream. We can't even protect our computers from malware and viruses, so how will we protect our fridges, watches and cars?' Write a comment on this statement, giving your own opinion about the security and usefulness of the Internet of Things.

1 WORKING WITH WORDS

Complete the crossword with the English equivalents of the German words. The words are all from exercise 1 on page 208 of the student's book.

1 montieren
2 Fähigkeiten
3 Oberfläche(nbehandlung)
4 Schicht
5 Scharnier
6 ersetzen
7 konstruieren, entwerfen
8 beweglich
9 Scheibchen
10 glatt
11 fest
12 Artikel, Gegenstand
13 winzig
14 Gegenstand, Objekt

2 LOOKING AT THE TEXT

→ Rezeption: Leseverstehen, SB S. 214

Read the text about 3D printing and then complete the diagram with words and phrases from the text.

HOW TO PRINT IN THREE DIMENSIONS

3D printing isn't very different from 2D printing. Just as an inkjet printer deposits ink on paper in two dimensions to create a flat image, a 3D printer deposits materials in three dimensions to create a solid shape. A 2D image is described by points on an x-axis and a y-axis; a 3D object has an additional z-axis.

3D printers can print in lots of different materials, such as polymers, metals and even concrete. There are three main 3D printing methods. These are stereolithography, fused deposition modelling and selective laser sintering.

Stereolithography uses a tank of liquid polymer, a vertically-movable platform and a computer-controlled ultraviolet (UV) laser. The polymer is photoreactive to UV light: it becomes hard where the UV light of the laser hits it. The printing process starts with the platform just below the surface of the polymer. The laser draws the base of the object in the surface of the polymer, forming a thin, solid layer. The platform moves down a little, then another layer is drawn – and so on, until the object is complete.

In fused deposition modelling, a spool of plastic filament or metal wire is the raw material. The computer-controlled, movable print head heats the material until it becomes soft, then squeezes out a tiny amount onto a static platform exactly where it is needed, drawing the object layer by layer. The print head can move in all three axes.

Selective laser sintering is similar to stereolithography but uses a fine powder as the raw material. This makes it possible to print objects in a range of materials, including glass, polymers and different metals. A thin layer of the powder is spread onto the platform. Then the laser draws the first slice of the object. Where the laser hits the powder, particles of the powder are heated rapidly and become fused together, or sintered. Then the platform moves down, another layer of powder is spread, the laser draws the next slice of the object, and so on.

(333 words)

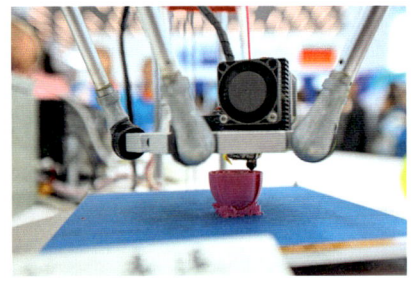

STEREOLITHOGRAPHY

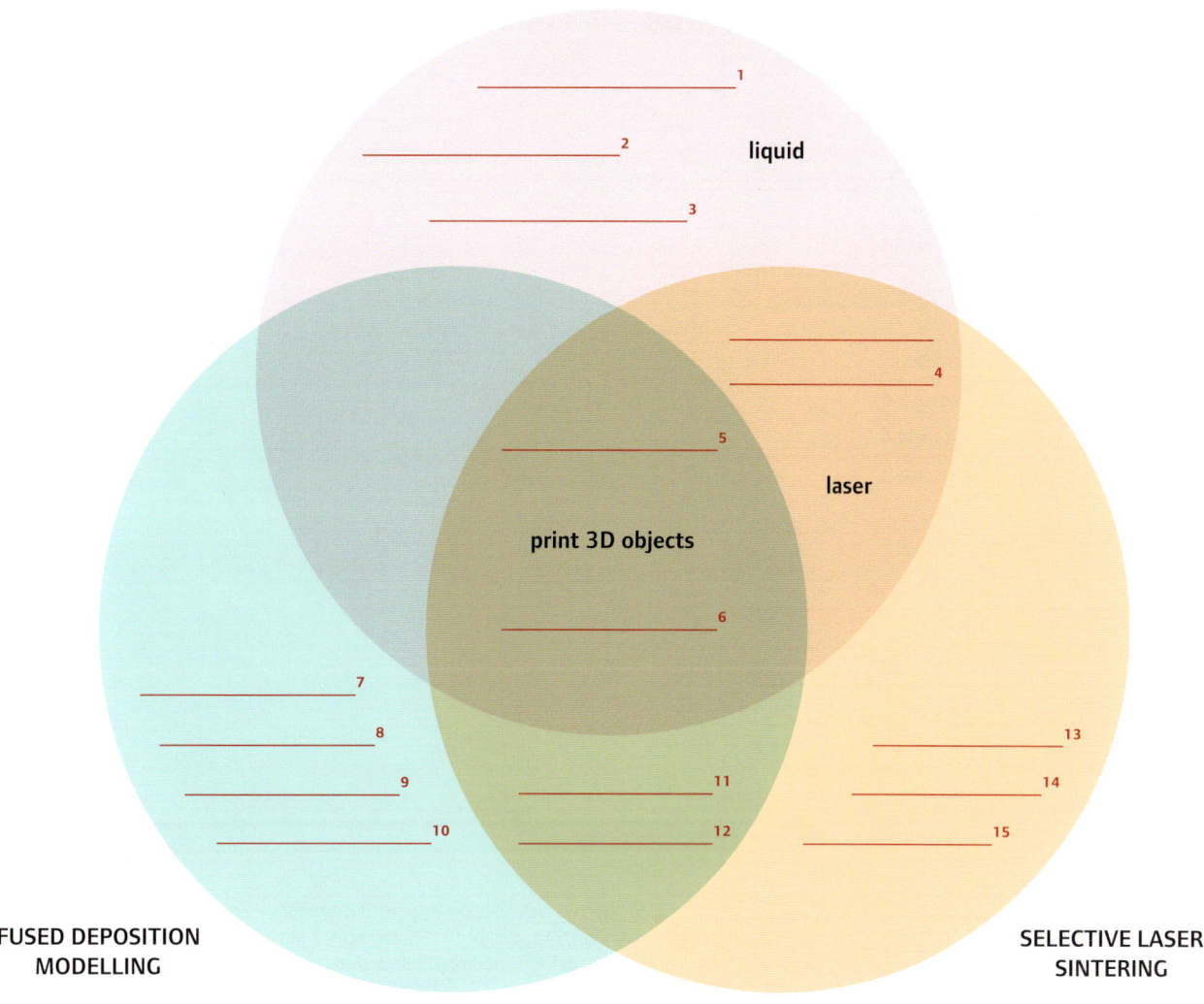

liquid

laser

print 3D objects

FUSED DEPOSITION
MODELLING

SELECTIVE LASER
SINTERING

3 3D PRINTING SOLUTIONS

Which 3D printing technique(s) would you use in these situations? Give reasons for your answers.

1 In zero gravity, e.g. on the International Space Station

_____

_____

_____

2 For printing car engine parts in small-volume manufacturing

_____

_____

_____

3 In an architect's office for making models of new buildings

_____

_____

_____

Track list

Track	Title/Exercise	Page
1	Title & credits	
2	Unit 1, Exercise 7B	6
3	Unit 2, Exercise 6	9
4	Unit 3, Exercise 4	11
5	Unit 5, Exercise 5	18
6	Unit 6, Exercise 3B	21
7	Unit 7, Exercise 6	27
8	Unit 8, Exercise 1	28
9	Unit 9, Exercise 5	34
10	Unit 10, Exercise 4	38
11	Unit 11, Exercise 4	42
12	Unit 12, Exercise 3	45
13	Unit 13, Exercise 4	49
14	Unit 14, Exercise 3	54
15	Unit 15, Exercise 5A	59
16	Unit 15, Exercise 5B	59
17	Unit 15, Exercise 5C	59
18	Unit 16, Exercise 4	62